Osoul Center
www.osoulcenter.com

EASE
AND TOLERANCE IN ISLAM

Abd Ar-Rahman bin
Abd Al-Kareem Ash-Sheha

King Fahd National Library Cataloging-in-Publication Data
Al-Sheha, Abdulrahman bin Abdul Kareem
Ease and Tolerance in Islam. / Abdulrahman bin Abdul Kareem
Al-Sheha.- Riyadh, 1438

68 p; 15.3 x 19.6 cm

ISBN: 978-81-19946-32-7

1- Preaching - Islam	I-Title
211 dc	1438/6148

L.D. no. 1438/6148
ISBN: 978-81-19946-32-7

In the name of Allah,
the Beneficent, the Merciful

Dear Reader,

Islam is a complete and integral Divine religion and way of life. It has a complete code of ethics for a happy life, as well as a peaceful and tranquil life after death. Islam is free from all imperfections and defects.

Any deviant or abnormal behavior observed in a Muslim should have no bearing on Islam, none whatsoever.

The reason for such deviant behavior is generally a poor understanding of the faith, and in other cases, weak faith that leads to the person going astray from what is proper and noble.

It is unjust and unreasonable for Islam to be assessed or evaluated based on any individuals' behavior or attitudes, with the exception of the Prophet Muhammad, who is the best example and role model for all humans.

TABLE OF CONTENTS

FOREWORD

مركز أصول
Osoul Center

+966 11 445 4900
+966 11 497 0126
P.O.Box 29465, Riyadh 11457
osoul@rabwah.sa
www.osoulcenter.com

All praise be to God, the Lord of all the worlds, the Creator of the heavens and earth and all creatures living in them. May God grant peace and blessings to Prophet Muhammad, God's final Messenger, whose message brought mercy to all mankind. May He also give His blessings to all the prophets and messengers whom He sent to guide mankind out of darkness and into light.

At the Osoul International Center for Islamic Advocacy, every new release that we produce gives us a great opportunity to interact with our readers. All our releases have the same overall objective; to present Islam to mankind, as it truly is. We aim to make people aware of Islam's fine aspects and profound teachings and to show clearly that it is the only faith that provides practical and effective solutions to all the problems faced by humanity. Islam gives clear and solid answers to all of the questions that have troubled people over many generations, such as: How did we come into existence and why do we exist? Where do we go from here? Furthermore, Islam is the only religion that requires its followers to love and respect all the prophets God sent, particularly Moses and Jesus (peace be upon them both).

We take great care to provide solid and rational proofs for our arguments, so as to give our readers the reassurance they need, and our releases also refute the accusations levelled against Islam and provide clarification to people's misunderstandings of Islamic teachings.

By God's grace, Islam is the fastest growing religion in our time, as confirmed by a study undertaken by the Pew Research Center(1), and our motive is to make this great divine faith known to all people.

This book, ***Ease and Tolerance in Islam***, explains that making things easy is a general feature of all aspects of the Islamic faith. Islam shuns the extreme attitudes of strictness that tend to prohibit what is lawful or casually permit that which God has made unlawful. It is a religion revealed by God and can be implemented by everyone, despite their different failings. People have their own feelings and abilities and Islamic law takes all this into account. Therefore, Islam addresses human nature and appeals to it, allowing everyone to practice it according to their different abilities. God says: "He has laid no hardship on you in anything that pertains to religion." (22: 78)

We hope that readers will find this book useful in adding to their knowledge and understanding of Islam.

Basil ibn Abdullah Al-Fawzan
Executive Director

(1) "The Future of the Global Muslim Population", Pew Research Center, 27 January 2011, Available at http://goo.gl/uk8y1i

01

INTRODUCTION

Islam is the religion that God revealed to all Prophets and Messengers, from the Prophet Adam, may God exalt his mention, to the Prophet Muhammad ﷺ(1). God, the Exalted, says: "Indeed, the religion in the sight of Allah is Islam." [3:19]

The last of all these prophets and messengers was Prophet Muhammad. He was sent after a long period of no prophet being sent to any people.

Each prophet called his people to the belief in the Oneness of God and to dedicate all acts of worship to God alone, without associating partners to Him. God, the Exalted, says:
"He has ordained for you of religion what He enjoined upon Noah and that which We have revealed to you, [O Muhammad], and what We enjoined upon Abraham and Moses and Jesus - to establish the religion and not be divided therein. Difficult for those who associate others with Allah is that to which you invite them. Allah chooses for Himself whom He wills and guides to Himself whoever turns back [to Him]."(42:13)

The prophets before the arrival of the Prophet Muhammad ﷺ were sent to their peoples exclusively; the laws that God gave them were significant to their specific period of time only. When a Prophet died and people deviated from the message they were given, God sent another prophet to guide them back to the Straight Path. This Prophet would once again guide the people to worshipping God alone and to not associating partners with Him. God, the Exalted, says:
"And We certainly sent into every nation a messenger, saying, 'Worship Allah and avoid idolatry.' And among them were those whom Allah guided, and among them were those upon whom error was [deservedly] decreed. So proceed through the earth and observe what was the end of those who denied the truth."(16:36)

The Message of Prophet Muhammad is also inclusive of all matters that relate to an individual, his society, and how to interact with those around him. It is also suitable for all times and places.

(1) This symbol means "may God exalt the mention of the Prophet and render him safe from all evil."

The last of all these prophets and messengers was the Prophet Muhammad ﷺ. He was sent after a long period of no prophets being sent to any people. He is the last of all Prophets and Messengers. His Message is the last of all divine messages to humankind. God, the Exalted, says:

"And We have not sent you except comprehensively to mankind as a bringer of good tidings and a warner. But most of the people do not know."(34:28)

The Islamic system of law is indeed a just system that is fair, easy to apply, and works to alleviate difficulties.

Due to the fact that this Message is the last message to humankind, it holds many distinguishing features that make it unlike previous messages. It holds accommodating rulings for all of the events that have come to pass and that will come to pass until the end of time. Allah, the Exalted, says:

"And We have not sent you, [O Muhammad], except as a mercy to the worlds."(21:107)

The Message of Prophet Muhammad ﷺ is also inclusive of all matters that relate to an individual, their society, and how to interact with those around them. It is also suitable for all times and places. Allah, the Exalted, says:

"This day I have perfected for you your religion and completed My favor upon you and have approved for you Islam as your religion."(5:3)

When a new situation arises that is not found in a previous age, a ruling is derived from one of the principles found in the Quran and Sunnah that is suitable to the situation.

Since tolerance is a distinguishing component of the Islamic faith, we will bring to light how this factor is the mainstay of all its rulings. Muslims are obliged to perform acts of worship to the best of their abilities. Allah, the Exalted, says:

"Allah does not charge a soul except with that within its capacity."(2:286)

The Prophet ﷺ said: "Adhere to what I have prescribed for you... If I forbid you from something, refrain from it, and if I order you with something, do of it as much as you can." (Bukhari)

The reason ease and tolerance are the foundations of the Islamic system of law is because it is a divine legal system, which takes

into consideration the emotional makeup of humanity and their abilities. Allah, the Exalted, says:
"He has chosen you and has not placed upon you in the religion any difficulty."(22:78)

The Islamic system of law is indeed a just system that is fair, easy to apply, and works to alleviate difficulties. When understood correctly, it is beloved to all who hear of it. It is a joy to put into practice, and even impartial non-Muslims have attested to this fact. Equality and fairness in the treatment of people is provided to all, regardless of wealth, age, or gender. Islam is a moderate system of law; no other system has equaled its moderation and beauty. Allah, the Exalted, says:
"And Allah wants to lighten for you [your difficulties], as mankind was created weak." (4:28)

Islam is a moderate system of law; no other system has equaled its moderation and beauty.

The justice in Islam is not only for Muslims, but rather is for those who are living amongst Muslims as well. Allah, the Exalted, says:
"Those who follow the Messenger, the unlettered prophet, whom they find written in what they have of the Torah and the Gospel, who enjoins upon them what is right and forbids them what is wrong and makes lawful for them the good things and prohibits for them the evil and relieves them of their burden and the shackles which were upon them. So they, who have believed in him, honored him, supported him and followed the light which was sent down with him - it is those who will be the successful." (7:157)

The justice in Islam is not only for Muslims, but rather is for those who are living amongst Muslims as well.

One degree of tolerance within the framework of Islamic law is that an individual is given flexibility to make personal decisions that are fitting in light of Islamic guidelines. This is very evident in the life story of the Prophet ﷺ. One example is the story of Muadth. The Prophet ﷺ sent Muadth, one of his companions, to Yemen. The Prophet asked him: "How will you judge?" He said: "I will judge by the commandments in the Book of Allah, and if I cannot find it therein, I will go to the Traditions of the

Messenger of Allah, and if I cannot find it therein, I will make an educated decision." The Prophet then placed his hand on his shoulder and said: "All praise is due to Allah for making it easy for the Messenger of Allah to choose the right individual for this post." (Abu Dawood)

In Islam, we are given general guidelines and principles with which we live our lives. When a new situation arises that is not found in a previous age, a ruling is derived from one of the principles found in the Quran and Sunnah that is suitable to the situation. Of these rules are the following:

01 The principle rule that governs the nature of all things is that they are lawful for use (unless proven otherwise).

02 A harmful matter should be removed and avoided.

03 Desperate needs legalize the unlawful.

04 A specific harm (that is individual) may be endured to avoid a greater harm.

There are many other rules similar to these which make it possible for Islamic law to adapt to all situations and places.

One degree of tolerance within the framework of Islamic law is that an individual is given flexibility to make personal decisions that are fitting in light of Islamic guidelines.

When a new situation arises that is not found in a previous age, a ruling is derived from one of the principles found in the Quran and Sunnah that is suitable to the situation.

02

ISLAM AND THE METHODOLOGY OF TOLERANCE

When we speak of tolerance in Islam, we are not speaking about a small component of the religion, but rather of a key feature of the Islamic faith. The Prophet ﷺ said: "The most beloved matter to Allah is the tolerant faith that matches the natural disposition of man." (Bukhari)

Islam is built upon a methodology of tolerance. Allah says:
"And thus we have made you a just community that you will be witnesses over the people and the Messenger will be a witness over you. And We did not make the direction in prayer which you used to face except that We might make evident who would follow the Messenger from who would turn back on his heels. And indeed, it is difficult except for those whom Allah has guided. And never would Allah have caused you to lose your faith. Indeed Allah is, to the people, Kind and Merciful." (2:143)

01 Islam is a tolerant faith in regards to political matters and foreign affairs. Muslims are ordered to behave in a just, impartial manner. Allah, the Exalted, says: "As regards those who do not fight you because of religion and do not expel you from your homes - Allah does not forbid you from being righteous toward them and acting justly toward them. Indeed, Allah loves those who act justly." (60:8)

02 Islam is tolerant in general societal matters, as well. One should not become arrogant towards others on account of their status in society. Allah, the Exalted, says: "O mankind, indeed We have created you from male and female and made you peoples and tribes that you may know one another. Indeed, the

When we speak of tolerance in Islam, we are not speaking about a small component of the religion, but rather of a key feature of the Islamic faith.

It should be known that when we speak of tolerance in Islam in relation to its various parts, we don't mean to say that one can purposely break the commandments and expect leniency and tolerance.

most noble of you in the sight of Allah is the most righteous of you. Indeed, Allah is Knowing and Acquainted."(49:13)

03 Islam is tolerant in terms of behavior and etiquette. It aims to cultivate within Muslims high standards and habits of manners and etiquette. Allah, the Exalted, says: "Take what is given freely, enjoin what is good, and turn away from the ignorant."(7:199)

Islam is tolerant in terms of behavior and etiquette. It aims to cultivate within Muslims high standards and habits of manners and etiquette.

Allah, the Exalted, also says: "Who spend for the sake of God during ease and hardship and who restrain anger and who pardon the people - and Allah loves the doers of good."(3:134)

Allah, the Exalted, also says: "And not equal are the good deed and the bad one. Repel evil by that [deed] which is better, and thereupon the one whom between you and him is enmity [will become] as though he was a devoted friend." (41:34)

04 Islam is also tolerant in relation to acts of worship. No one is overburdened, and those who put forth an effort towards worship will be rewarded graciously for their efforts. Allah, the Exalted, says: "But those who believed and did righteous deeds - We charge no soul except [within] its capacity. Those are the companions of Paradise; they will abide therein eternally."(7:42)

Islam is also tolerant in relation to acts of worship. No one is overburdened, and those who put forth an effort towards worship will be rewarded graciously for their efforts.

05 Islam is tolerant in terms of economy. All means through which one could be oppressed through finances is forbidden. Allah, the Exalted, says: "Those who consume interest cannot stand [on the Day of Resurrection] except as one stands who is being beaten by Satan into insanity. That is because they say, 'Trade is [just] like interest' But Allah has permitted trade and has forbidden interest. So whoever has received an admonition from his Lord and desists may have what is past, and his affair rests with Allah. But whoever returns to [dealing in interest or usury] - those are the companions of the Fire; they will abide eternally therein."(2:275)

06 Islam is tolerant in terms of education and training. The Prophet ﷺ said: "Give the good news, and do not make things difficult." (Ibn Hibban)

The textual passages of Islam, time and time again, reaffirm the methodology of tolerance by putting it into practice. The Prophet ﷺ said: "Ease is not placed into something except that it would beautify it, and it would not be removed from something except that it would blemish it." (Muslim)

The Prophet ﷺ said: "O Allah, whoever is given charge over my community and they make it difficult for others, make their lives difficult. And whoever makes things easy for others, make things easy for them." (Muslim)

The textual passages of Islam, time and time again, reaffirm the methodology of tolerance by putting it into practice.

Whoever is tolerant will be blessed with entry into heaven and receive protection from the Hell-Fire. The Prophet ﷺ said: "Whoever is easy going, soft-hearted and near to Allah, he would be forbidden from entering Hell." (At-Targheeb wat-Tarheeb)

It should be known that when we speak of tolerance in Islam, it doesn't mean that one can purposely break the commandments under the guise of leniency.

A'ishah, may Allah be pleased with her, said: "The Prophet was not given a choice between two matters except that he chose the easier of the two, except if it was a sinful course of action, in which case, he would distance himself from it." (Muslim)

The exception to this rule is in circumstances of dire need or necessity, wherein some actions which are otherwise considered sinful may be pardoned or overlooked due to no other option being available.

It should be known that when we speak of tolerance in Islam, it doesn't mean that one can purposely break the commandments under the guise of leniency.

THE TOLERANCE OF ISLAM IN TERMS OF BELIEF:

The beliefs of Islam are the cornerstone aspect of the Islamic faith. It is something that cannot be done away with under any circumstances. Allah, the Exalted, says:
"Indeed, Allah does not forgive associating partners with Him in worship, but He forgives what is less than that for whom He wills. And he who associates in worship others with Allah has certainly fabricated a tremendous sin."(4:48)

THE ASPECT OF EASE IN THE ISLAMIC FAITH:

01 It is a clear faith with no difficulties in understanding it.

All the followers of Islam are obliged to accept and believe that the Messengers and Prophets of Allah were all sent by God with the message of belief in the Oneness of God.

02 All the followers of Islam are obliged to accept and believe that the Messengers and Prophets of Allah were all sent by God with the message of belief in the Oneness of God. Allah, the Exalted, says:

"The Messenger has believed in what was revealed to him from his Lord, and [so have] the believers. All of them have believed in Allah and His angels and His books and His messengers, [saying], 'We make no distinction between any of His messengers.' And they say, 'We hear and we obey. [We seek] Your forgiveness, our Lord, and to You is the [final] destination.'"(2:285)

03 No one is forced into Islam. Allah, the Exalted, says:

"There shall be no compulsion in [acceptance of] the religion. The right course has become clear from the wrong. So whoever disbelieves in idolatry and believes in Allah has grasped the most trustworthy handhold with no break in it. And Allah is Hearing and Knowing."(2:256)

Whoever the Message of Islam has reached, and to whom it was clarified, would have the choice of choosing their faith, either to accept or reject the Message.

No one has the right to force anyone into Islam. Allah, the Exalted, says:

"And had your Lord willed, those on earth would have believed - all of them entirely. Then, [O Muhammad], would you compel the people in order that they become believers?"(10:99)

Whoever the Message of Islam has reached, and to whom it was clarified, would have the choice of choosing their faith, either to accept or reject the Message. Allah, the Exalted, says:

"And say, 'The truth is from your Lord, so whoever wills - let him believe; and whoever wills - let him disbelieve.' Indeed, We have prepared for the wrongdoers a fire whose walls will surround them. And if they call for relief, they will be relieved with water like murky oil, which scalds [their] faces. Wretched is the drink, and evil is the resting place."(18:29)

04 Another aspect of its tolerance is that a person is judged by Allah for what they do. One should not try to decipher the inward meanings of someone's actions and judge them based on that. Instead, Muslims are ordered by Allah to judge others based on what we witness ourselves.

Tolerance is that a person is judged by Allah for what they do. One should not try to decipher the inward meanings of someone's actions and judge them based on that.

As we established above, a person is judged by what he does and what is apparent from his actions. This is also established in this narration of the Prophet ﷺ:

"'Ali bin Abi Talib sent a piece of gold, not yet taken out of its ore, in a tanned leather satchel to the Messenger of Allah ﷺ. The Messenger ﷺ distributed that amongst four people... On that, one of his companions said, 'We are more deserving of this gold than these people.' When that news reached the Prophet ﷺ, he said, 'Don't you trust me, as I am the one who receives the Divine Revelation from God?' There got up a man with sunken eyes, raised cheekbones, raised forehead, a thick beard, a shaven head and a waist sheet that was tucked up and he said, 'O Allah's Messenger! Fear Allah!' The Prophet ﷺ said, 'Woe to you! Am I not of all the people of the earth the most entitled to fear Allah?' Then that man went away. Khalid bin Waleed (may Allah be pleased with him) said: 'O Messenger of Allah, give me permission to strike his neck.' The Prophet ﷺ said, 'No, for he may offer prayers.' Khalid said, 'Numerous are those who offer prayers and say by their tongues (i.e. mouths) what is not in their hearts.' The Messenger of Allah ﷺ said, 'I have not been ordered (by Allah) to search the hearts of the people or cut open their bellies.'" (Bukhari)

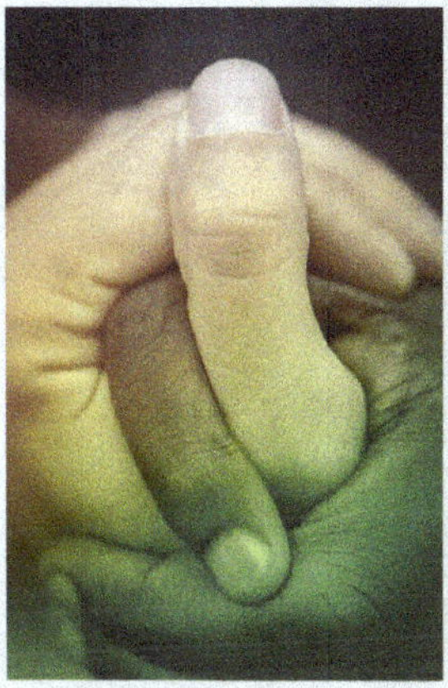

When one is put in a situation and is threatened with harm, then in that case he may take the necessary steps to protect himself.

05 When one is put in a situation and is threatened with harm, then in that case he may take the necessary steps to protect himself. Allah, the Exalted, says:

"Whoever disbelieves in Allah after his belief... except for one who is forced [to renounce his religion] while his heart is secure in faith. But those who [willingly] open their souls to disbelief, upon them is wrath from Allah, and for them is a great punishment." (16:106)

Ammar bin Yasir, one of the Companions, was in a life and death situation, where he was almost killed by those non-Muslims who were torturing him. He was asked by those who tortured him to speak ill of the Prophet ﷺ in order to save himself further torture, so he did that. He was so saddened by what he had done. The Prophet ﷺ consoled him and said: "How is your faith?" He said, "I am content with Islam." The Prophet ﷺ then said: "If they want to torture you again, say what you must." (Ibn Kathir)

Islam has also freed humankind from giving servitude to other humans and delivered them to worshipping God alone.

06 Islam has also freed humankind from giving servitude to other humans and it has delivered them to worshiping God alone. Allah, the Exalted, says:

"But they have taken besides Him gods which create nothing, while they themselves are created, and possess not for themselves any harm or benefit and possess not [power to cause] death or life or resurrection." (25:3)

Allah, the Exalted, says:

"And if Allah should touch you with adversity, there is no remover of it except Him, and if He intends for you good, then there is none to repel His bounty. He causes it to reach whom He wills of His servants. And He is the Forgiving, the Merciful." (10:107)

To avoid any unnecessary veneration towards any individual, Allah clarifies that the Prophet Muhammad is merely a man, as were all the prophets before him. They were merely men, who deserved no excessive veneration or deification. Allah, the Exalted, says:

To avoid any unnecessary veneration towards any individual, Allah clarifies that the Prophet Muhammad is merely a man, as were all the prophets before him.

"Say, 'I myself have no power to benefit or do harm, save as God pleases. If I had knowledge of the unseen, I would have availed myself of an abundance of good, and no harm would have touched me. I am but a warner and a bearer of good tidings for those who will believe.'" (7:188)

07 Allah as well orders Muslims to be fair and just towards all people, regardless of their faith, religion, color, ethnic background, or societal status. Allah, the Exalted, says:
"Indeed, God orders justice and good conduct and giving to relatives and forbids immorality and bad conduct and oppression. He admonishes you that perhaps you will be reminded." (16:90)

One should be fair to others whether you might be in a happy or angry mood, with Muslims or with non-Muslims. Allah, the Exalted, says:
"O you who have believed, persistently stand firm for Allah, witnesses in justice, and do not let the hatred of a people prevent you from being just. Be just; that is nearer to righteousness. And fear Allah; indeed, Allah is acquainted with what you do." (4:135)

A sign of the tolerance in the Islamic Faith is that a Muslim believes that all people have been favored by God.

08 A sign of the tolerance in the Islamic Faith is that a Muslim believes that all people have been favored by God. Allah, the Exalted, says:
"And We have certainly honored the children of Adam and carried them on the land and sea and provided for them of the good things and preferred them over much of what We have created, with [definite] preference."(17:70)

Qais ibn Sa'd reported: "A funeral passed by the Messenger of Allah ﷺ, and he stood up. It was said to him, 'It is a Jew.' The Prophet replied, 'Was he not a soul?'" (Bukhari)

In reality, the Shari'ah simply denotes the divine system of Law given to humankind. It is a system that is built on tolerance and ease.

THE TOLERANCE OF ISLAM IN RELATION TO SHARI'AH:

Nowadays, the term "Shari'ah" invokes archaic images of lashings and other public punishments. In reality, the Shari'ah simply denotes the divine system of Law given to humankind. It is a system that is built on tolerance and ease. Here are a few points to keep in mind:

01 The textual passages in the Quran and Sunnah (Prophetic

Tradition) are very easy to understand. Allah, the Exalted, says: "And We have indeed made the Qur'an easy to understand and remember, so is there any who will [receive admonition and] remember?"(54:17)

The textual passages are very clear in their meaning; there is no difficulty in understanding what is meant by the text. If there is a situation where one is in doubt, God directs us to ask those who have knowledge. He says: "So ask the people of the message if you do not know." (16:43)

The textual passages in the Quran and Sunnah (Prophetic Tradition) are very easy to understand.

This is indeed an important aspect. If someone lacks the knowledge on how to solve a worldly problem, they would have to ask specialists in that area to help them resolve that particular situation. The same applies to questions of religion. God has ordained that speaking without knowledge is a grave sin. Whoever speaks in religion without knowledge, and then forbids a lawful matter or vice versa, has committed a major sin. God, the Exalted, says: "Say, 'My Lord has only forbidden immoralities - what is apparent of them and what is concealed - and sin, and oppression without right, and that you associate with Allah that for which He has not sent down authority, and that you say about Allah that which you do not know.'" (7:33)

God has ordained that speaking without knowledge is a grave sin. Whoever speaks in religion without knowledge, and then forbids a lawful matter or vice versa, has committed a major sin.

The Messenger of Allah ﷺ clarified the negative consequences of one who is not knowledgeable speaking without knowledge. He would surely mislead himself and others. The Prophet ﷺ said: "God does not remove knowledge from his slaves by causing them to forget it; rather, knowledge would be lost by the loss of scholars. Until there will remain no scholar, then people would appoint over themselves ignorant individuals and they would issue judgments without knowledge and mislead themselves and others." (Bukhari)

There are no mysterious or unexplained issues in Islam. At times there are issues that pertain to the unseen world that we will not have a complete grasp over; in reality, they would not affect one's faith, nor bring any benefit. One such issue is, as

God says, "And they ask you, [O Muhammad], about the soul. Say, 'The soul is of the affair of my Lord. And mankind have not been given of knowledge except a little.'" (17:85)

Allah, the Exalted, also says: "They ask you, [O Muhammad], about the Hour, when will it be established? Say, 'Its knowledge is only with my Lord. None will reveal its time except Him. Heavy is its burden through the heavens and the earth. It will not come upon you except unexpectedly.' They ask you as if you are familiar with it. Say, 'Its knowledge is only with Allah, but most of the people do not know.'" (7:187)

There are no mysterious or unexplained issues in Islam. At times there are issues that pertain to the unseen world that we will not have a complete grasp over.

All that will benefit us in terms of knowledge that is related to the unseen world has already been explained to us by our Prophet ﷺ. These include the descriptions of Heaven and Hell, and the stories of the previous nations so that we can reflect upon what happened to them. Allah, the Exalted, says:
"So I have warned you of a Fire which is blazing. None will [enter to] burn therein except the most wretched one. Who had denied and turned away. But the righteous one will avoid it - [He] who gives [from] his wealth to purify himself. And not [giving] for anyone who has [done him] a favor to be rewarded, but only seeking the countenance of his Lord, Most High. And he is going to be satisfied."(92:14-21)

02 Unlike man-made laws, which may be applicable to some while exempted by others due to loopholes, the laws of Islam are divine. The Law of God is final and definite, and it is the law to which all would refer, be they rich or poor, noble or ignoble. Allah, the Exalted, says:
"It is not for a believing man or a believing woman, when Allah and His Messenger have decided a matter, that they should [thereafter] have any choice about their affair. And whoever disobeys Allah and His Messenger has certainly strayed into clear error."(33:36)

The laws of Islam are divine. The Law of God is final and definite, and is the law to which all would refer, be they rich or poor, noble or ignoble.

Allah has ordained that all should respect and uphold this system of law. Allah, the Exalted, says: "The only statement of the [true] believers when they are called to Allah and His Messenger to judge between them is that they say, 'We hear and we obey.' And those are the successful."(24:51)

No one in Islam has absolute authority, including the president or leader; he is subject to the same laws as everyone else. This is the beauty and tolerance of Islam. No one can transgress these rules and boundaries. The Prophet ﷺ said: "A Muslim must listen and obey their leader, except when ordered with a sinful matter. In that case, there is no obedience." (Bukhari)

Another aspect of the divine laws of God is that they are not susceptible to change and do not become outdated.

03 Another aspect of the divine laws of God is that they are not susceptible to change and do not become outdated like man-made laws. These laws are absolute for all times and places. God has decreed the divine system of law and it does not change. God, the Exalted, says: "Then is it the judgment of [the time of] ignorance they desire? But who is better than Allah in judgment for a people who are certain [in faith]."(5:50)

04 In Islam, there is no structure of priesthood, nor are there infallible men whose opinions are regarded above the word of God. Allah says: "Unquestionably, for Allah is the pure religion. And those who take protectors besides Him [say], 'We only worship them that they may bring us nearer to Allah in position.'" (39:3)

In Islam there is no clergy structure, nor are there infallible men whose opinions are regarded above the word of God.

No one has the power to harm or benefit. This is something exclusive to God alone. Allah, the Exalted, says:

"Indeed, those you worship besides Allah are only servants like you. So call upon them and let them respond to you, if you should be truthful."(7:194)

Islam stresses that every individual has a direct link to God; there are no intermediaries between us and Him. He forgives our sins and grants us what we wish. Allah, the Exalted, says: "And whoever does a wrong or wrongs himself but then seeks forgiveness of Allah will find Allah Forgiving and Merciful." (4:110) Allah, the Exalted, also says: "Call upon Me, and I will respond to you."(40:60)

In Islam, there are no religious authorities that can legalize what is unlawful or prohibit that which is lawful, for the right of law-making belongs to God alone. It is a known fact that among previous nations, the law was often changed to suit the whims and fancies of people in power. God, the Exalted, says about this: "They have taken their scholars and monks as lords besides Allah." (9:31)

When their rabbis and priests legalized something that was unlawful, or did the opposite, their people would follow and obey them. This is undoubtedly an aspect of worship!

Islam stresses that every individual has a direct link to God; there are no intermediaries between us and Him.

05 Another aspect of Islam's tolerance is that there is a system known as Shura, or mutual consultation. This is used in cases wherein there is a public benefit to be earned; where people of knowledge and expertise in a certain field can be consulted to take the best course of action. Allah says: "So by mercy from Allah, [O Muhammad], you were lenient with them. And if you had been rude [in speech] and harsh in heart, they would have disbanded from about you. So pardon them and ask forgiveness for them and consult them in the matter. And when you have decided, then rely upon Allah. Indeed, Allah loves those who rely [upon Him]."(3:159)

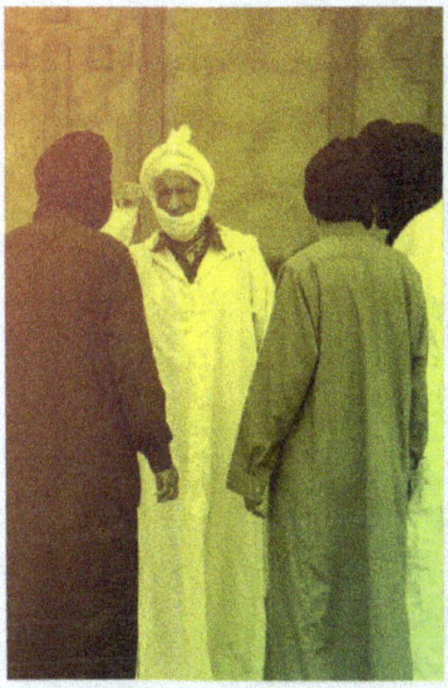

Shura is used in cases wherein there is a public benefit to be earned, where people of knowledge and expertise in a certain field can be consulted to take the best course of action.

06 Islam has also opened the gateway for Ijtihad, which is when a scholar of expertise would exert his effort to reach a ruling in a certain matter that may not be directly mentioned in the Scriptural texts. In Islam, the general guidelines are given and one is to uphold them when a situation arises. This makes the laws of Islam versatile and fitting for all places and times.

07 God has ordained laws to protect all communities from extremism. Allah, the Exalted, says:
"Allah intends for you ease and does not intend for you hardship." (2:185)

The Prophet ﷺ said: "Beware of extremism, for this is what destroyed the previous nations." (Nasaee')

The Prophet ﷺ preached a moderate way of life. Anas bin Malik said: "Three people came to the houses of the Prophet ﷺ asking how he spent his days and how he worshipped Allah. When they were informed of what the Prophet ﷺ did of worship, they saw it as little, so they said: 'The Prophet has been forgiven by Allah, who are we to compare ourselves to him?' One said: 'As for I, I will pray continuously throughout the night and forsake sleep.' The second said: 'I will fast for the rest of my days.' The third said: 'As for me, I will never get married.' The Prophet ﷺ came by afterwards and asked, are you the ones who said this and this? He said: 'Indeed I am the most God-fearing amongst you and yet I pray at night and also rest, I fast and break my fast, and I marry women. Whoever does not want to adhere to my way is not from me.'" (Bukhari)

The Prophet made a point of guiding his companions to the moderate path in life so that they would not fall into extremism.

Islam is a moderate way of life. It strikes a beautiful balance between this worldly life and the Next.

The Prophet ﷺ made a point of guiding his companions to the moderate path in life so that they would not fall into extremism. It is narrated in the hadeeth[1] of Abdullah bin Amr bin al-Aas that the Prophet ﷺ said to him: "(Is it true) that you fast all day and stand in prayer all night?" The companion replied that the report was indeed true. The Prophet then said: "Do not do that! Observe the fast sometimes and also leave (it) at other times. Stand up for prayer at night and also sleep at night. Your body has a right over you, your eyes have a right over you and your wife has a right over you. Fast three days a month as the reward of good deeds is multiplied ten times and that will be equal to one year of fasting." I replied, "I have more power than that." The Prophet said to me, "Then fast one day and give up fasting for a day and that is the fasting of Prophet David (Dawud) and that is the best fasting." I replied, "I have more power than that." The Prophet said, "There is no better fasting than that." (Bukhari)

The Prophet ﷺ also said: "Whoever fasts daily throughout his life is just as the one who does not fast at all." (Bukhari)

(1) One of various reports describing the words, actions, or habits of the Prophet Muhammad. Considered an aspect of the revelation from God.

This does not mean that Islam encourages one to seek the pleasures of this life while disregarding the Next Life. Rather, Islam is a moderate way of life. It strikes a beautiful balance between this worldly life and the Next.

Allah, the Exalted, says:
"O you who have believed, when the call to prayer is heard for the prayer on the day of Friday, then proceed to the remembrance of Allah and leave trade. That is better for you, if you only knew." (62:9)

In light of a person's worldly needs, Allah has ordered that one not forget about his need for sustenance. He, the Exalted, says: "And when the prayer has been concluded, disperse within the land and seek from the bounty of Allah, and remember Allah often that you may succeed." (62:10)

Allah has also ordered us to avoid being wasteful. He, the Exalted, says:
"O Children of Adam, dress properly and well whenever you are at worship, and eat and drink but do not be wasteful. God does not like the wasteful." (7:31)

08 Another sign of tolerance in Islam is when a person fears his demise or that harm shall befall him, it is lawful for him to consume that which is otherwise unlawful so that he may sustain himself and stay alive. Allah, the Exalted, says:
"He has only forbidden to you dead animals, blood, the flesh of swine, and that which has been dedicated to other than Allah. But whoever is forced [by necessity], neither desiring [it] nor transgressing [its limit], there is no sin upon him. Indeed, Allah is Forgiving and Merciful." (2:173)

In one of the commentaries of the Qur'an, it explains: "It is the set of laws and beliefs that marks a man as a man and not an animal, or an angel or a devil. It takes into consideration ones abilities and complete capabilities as well as the human weakness."

09 Another sign of the tolerance of Islam is that one's good

Another sign of tolerance in Islam is when a person fears his demise or that harm shall befall him, it is lawful for him to consume that which is unlawful so that he may sustain himself and stay alive.

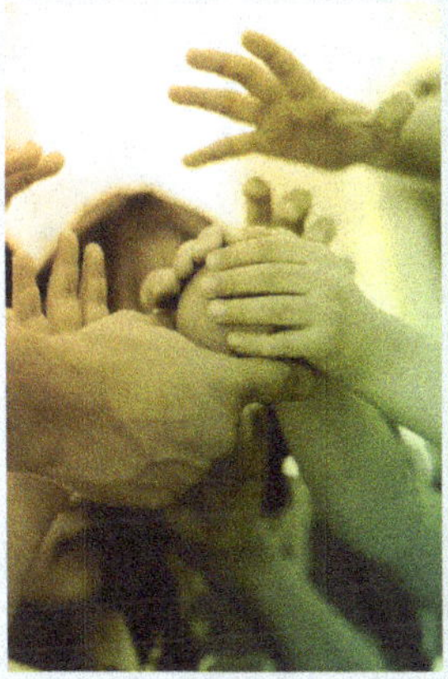

Another sign of the tolerance of Islam is that one's good deeds would be multiplied many times over.

deeds would be multiplied many times over. Allah, the Exalted, says: "Whoever comes [on the Day of Judgment] with a good deed will have ten times the like thereof [to his credit], and whoever comes with an evil deed will not be recompensed except the like thereof, and they will not be wronged." (6:160)

Islam is a world faith, and it is for all people in all times and places. In light of this, calling people to Islam and propagating the true faith must be done in a manner that is ethical, and in a good way.

TOLERANCE OF ISLAM IN TERMS OF CALLING OTHERS TO ISLAM

Islam is a world faith, and it is for all people in all times and places. In light of this, calling people to Islam and propagating the true faith must be done in a manner that is ethical, and in a good way so that the others who are called to it will accept it and think of it in an impartial way. Allah, the Exalted, says:

"Invite to the way of your Lord with wisdom and good instruction, and dialogue with them in the best manner. Indeed, your Lord is most knowing of who has strayed from His way, and He is most knowing of who is [rightly] guided." (16:125)

Let us discuss some of the aspects of tolerance when it comes to propagating Islam.

01 We accept people of all other faiths, regardless of their past. Amr ibn al-Aas, a man who had fought against the Prophet ﷺ and his Companions for years, said: "When Allah put Islam in my heart, I came to the Prophet ﷺ and said, 'Give me your right hand so that I may swear allegiance to you.'" He held out his hand but then I withdrew my hand. He said, "What is the matter, Amr?" I said, "I want to stipulate a condition." He said, "What do you want to stipulate?" I said, "That I will be forgiven". He said, "Do you not know that Islam destroys that which came before it?" (Muslim)

Another aspect of Islam's tolerance in terms of propagating Islam is that one who calls others to the faith should do so in a good manner.

02 Another aspect of Islam's tolerance in terms of propagating Islam is that one who calls others to the faith should do so in a good, inviting manner. The Prophet ﷺ said: "Give glad-tidings, and do not push people away. Make matters easy and do not make them difficult." (Muslim)

03 We are asked to discuss respectfully with those who hold opinions that are not congruent with ours. Allah, the Exalted, says:

"And do not argue with the People of the Scripture except in a way that is best, except for those who commit injustice among them, and say, 'We believe in that which has been revealed to us and revealed to you. And our God and your God is one; and we are Muslims [in submission] to Him.'" (29:46)

No one can force another to accept their opinion, nor can anyone persuade another forcefully.

No one can force another to accept their opinion. The Islamic view is that faith stems from the heart and as such you can never force faith into someone's heart against their will; they must choose it. Let us look at the story of Al-Aas bin Wa'il. He was a pagan who refused to accept the faith of Islam. He went to the Messenger of Allah ﷺ with a bone that was decomposed and he crushed it and said to the Prophet ﷺ: "Do you claim we shall be resurrected after we turn into this?" He said, "Yes. Allah will cause you to die, then resurrect you and then put you into the Hell-Fire." He then recited the words of God:

"And he presents for Us an example and forgets his [own] creation. He says, 'Who will give life to bones while they are disintegrated?' Say, 'He will give them life who produced them the first time, and He is, of all creation, Knowing.' [It is] He who made for you from the green tree, fire, and then from it you ignite. Is not He who created the heavens and the earth Able to create the likes of them? Yes, [it is so], and He is the Knowing Creator. His command is only when He intends a thing that He says to it, 'Be,' and it is. So exalted is He in whose hand is the realm of all things, and to Him you will be returned." (36:78-83)

The Islamic view is that faith stems from the heart and as such you can never force faith into someone's heart against their will; they must choose it.

Arguments of this nature make it impossible for one to refute the truth. Another example is what is mentioned in the Quran regarding a discussion that took place between King Nimrod and the Prophet Abraham. Allah, the Exalted, says:

"Have you not considered the one who argued with Abraham about his Lord [merely] because Allah had given him kingship?

When Abraham said, 'My Lord is the one who gives life and causes death.' He said, 'I give life and cause death.' Abraham said, 'Indeed, Allah brings up the sun from the east, so bring it up from the west.' So the disbeliever was overwhelmed [by astonishment], and Allah does not guide the wrongdoing people." (2:258)

Another aspect of the tolerance of Islam is that one should not rile people up, spread hatred or cause commotion.

04 Another aspect of the tolerance of Islam is that one should not rile people up, spread hatred or cause commotion. Allah, the Exalted, says:
"And tell My servants to say that which is best. Indeed, Satan induces [dissension] among them. Indeed Satan is ever, to mankind, a clear enemy." (17:53)

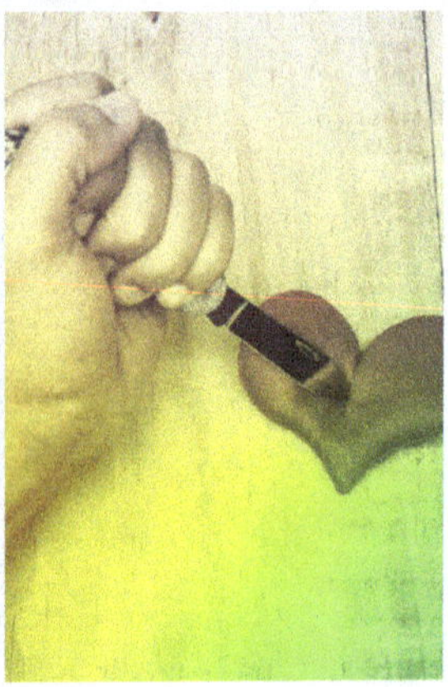

05 We use methods to draw people to Islam that will help them love Islam. The Messenger of Allah ﷺ said: "If anyone wrongs a non-Muslim citizen, usurps his rights, burdens him with more work than he is able to do or takes something from him without his consent, I will plead for him (the non-Muslim citizen) on the Day of Resurrection." (Abu Dawud)

06 We should be very gentle, kind and accepting. Allah says:

"Go, both of you, to Pharaoh. Indeed, he has transgressed. And speak to him with gentle speech that perhaps he may be reminded or fear [Allah]." (20:43-4)

We always ask that those who differ with us in an argument bring forth their evidences and proofs.

07 We always ask that those who differ with us in an argument to bring forth their evidences and proofs. Allah, the Exalted, says:
"Say, [O Muhammad], 'Have you considered that which you invoke besides Allah? Show me what they have created of the earth. Or did they have partnership in the creation of the heavens? Bring me a scripture [revealed] before this or a [remaining] trace of knowledge, if you should be truthful.'" (46:4)

08 We are asked to discuss topics in constructive ways. Allah, the Exalted, says:
"Say, 'O People of the Scripture, come to a word that is equitable between us and you - that we will not worship except Allah and

not associate anything with Him and not take one another as lords instead of Allah.' But if they turn away, then say, 'Bear witness that we are Muslims [submitting to Him].'" (3:64)

09 Whoever accepts Islam will become sin-free, in the sight of God, upon becoming Muslim. He will bear no sins from his past life. Allah, the Exalted, says:
"Say to those who have disbelieved [that] if they cease, what has previously occurred will be forgiven for them. But if they return [to hostility] - then the precedent of the former [rebellious] peoples has already taken place." (8:38)

Whoever accepts Islam will become sin-free, in the sight of God, upon becoming Muslim.

10 Anyone who becomes a Muslim will receive the reward of all the good things they had done in the past, before they accepted Islam. Hakim bin Hizam said: "O Messenger of Allah! What do you think about my good deeds which I used to do during the period of ignorance (before embracing Islam) like keeping good relations with my kin, freeing slaves and giving charity, etc. Will I receive the reward for those deeds?" The Messenger of Allah ﷺ said, "You have embraced Islam with all those good deeds which you did." (Bukhari)

Anyone who becomes a Muslim will receive the reward of all the good things they had done in the past, before they accepted Islam.

11 Whoever accepts Islam from a previous religion will receive their reward two fold. Allah, the Exalted, says: "Those will be given their reward twice for what they patiently endured and [because] they avert evil through good, and from what We have provided them they spend." (28:54)

TOLERANCE OF ISLAM TOWARDS NON-MUSLIMS:

Before we begin, let us mention the words of the award winning TED speaker and author Dr. Karen Armstrong: "Ever since the Crusades, when Christians from western Europe were fighting holy wars against Muslims in the near east, western people have often perceived Islam as a violent and intolerant faith - even though when this prejudice took root Islam had a better record of tolerance than Christianity."

All financial transactions are lawful between Muslims and non-Muslims, such as buying and selling homes and cars,and taking part in companies, as long as the Islamic principles are upheld.

It is lawful for non-Muslims to enter the Masjid, if there is a need. This provision does not include the Grand Mosque in Makkah.

01 All financial transactions are lawful between Muslims and non-Muslims, such as buying and selling, and taking part in companies, as long as the Islamic principles are upheld. A'ishah, may Allah be pleased with her said: "The Prophet ﷺ bought some food from a Jewish seller and was not able to pay the money upfront so he left his armor as collateral with him until he could pay." (Bukhari)

The only form of bartering that is unlawful is that which contains a degree of harm. Allah, the Exalted, says:
"O you who have believed, do not consume usury, doubled and multiplied, but fear Allah that you may be successful." (3:130)

Allah, the Exalted, also says:
"O you who have believed, indeed, Intoxicants, gambling, sacrificing on stone alters, and divining arrows are but defilement from the work of Satan, so avoid it that you may be successful. Satan only wants to cause between you animosity and hatred through intoxicants and gambling and to distract you from the remembrance of Allah and from prayer. So will you not desist?" (5:90-91)

02 It is lawful for Muslims to perform prayers in a non-Muslim place of worship. Abu Musa performed prayers in a church in Damascus.

It is not praiseworthy for a Muslim to do this, for there maybe idols, and other pictures. So, it is recommended that only if a person cannot find any other place to pray in, he may pray there. Umar said to a Christian, "We do not enter your Churches due to the pictures that are posted on the walls."

03 It is lawful for non-Muslims to enter the Masjid, if there is a need. This provision does not include the Grand Mosque in Makkah. As for Madinah, the Prophet ﷺ met with some non-Muslim delegates there.

04 It is good for Muslims to visit non-Muslims who are sick and

to supplicate for them that they become healthy. Anas said a young boy from a Jewish background fell sick and the Prophet ﷺ visited him and encouraged him to accept Islam. The boy looked to his father for permission, and the father told his sick son: "Obey Abal-Qasim (i.e. Muhammad ﷺ)", so he said the Testimony of Faith and the Prophet ﷺ said, "All praise is due to Allah who saved him from the Fire." (Bukhari)

It is lawful for Muslims to visit the non-Muslims who are sick and to make dua (i.e. supplicate) for them that they become healthy.

05 We can also give our condolences to non-Muslims. Abu Hurairah said that the Prophet ﷺ said: "I sought permission to visit my mother's grave and it was granted to me." (Muslim).

06 One can give charity to non-Muslims as long as they are not engaged in oppressing others. Abdullah Bin 'Amr slaughtered a sheep and gave some of its meat as a gift to his Jewish neighbor. He said, "The Messenger of Allah ﷺ said: 'The Angel Gabriel kept on enjoining the good treatment of neighbors to the extent that I thought that he would include neighbors as heirs.'" (Muslim)

07 Islam has further encouraged Muslims to maintain the relations of kinship even if they be non-Muslims. Asma bint Abi Bakr, came to the Prophet ﷺ and said: "My mother is visiting me and she is a non-Muslim." He said, "Be kind to your mother." (Bukhari)

Islam has allowed a Muslim to maintain the relations of his family even if they be non-Muslims.

08 There is no concern for Muslims to eat from non-Muslims utensils and use their clothes as long as they are not made from materials that are unlawful for us. Abu Tha'labah al-Khushani said: "O Messenger of Allah, we are in a land that belongs to the People of the Book, shall we eat with their utensils?" He said: "If you can find other utensils, it is better. If not, then wash them and use them." (Bukhari)

09 It is also lawful for a Muslim man to marry a chaste woman from the People of the Book. Allah, the Exalted, says:
"This day [all] good foods have been made lawful, and the food of those who were given the Scripture is lawful for you and your food is lawful for them. And lawful in marriage are chaste women from among the believers and chaste women from

among those who were given the Scripture before you, when you have given them their due compensation, desiring chastity, not unlawful sexual intercourse or taking them as [secret] lovers. And whoever denies the faith, his work has become worthless, and he, in the Hereafter, will be among the losers." (5:5)

10 Whoever accepts Islam and is married to a woman from the People of the Book, his marriage would continue to remain valid.

It is lawful for a Muslim man to marry a chaste woman from the People of the Book.

11 It is lawful for one to eat of the foods slaughtered by the People of the Book, as long as it is lawful for us to eat and they have mentioned the name of God over it. Allah, the Exalted, says:
"And do not eat of that upon which the name of God has not been mentioned, for indeed, it is grave disobedience." (6:121)

It is lawful for one to eat of the foods slaughtered by the People of the Book.

12 We are to offer protection to a non-Muslim if he seeks it. Allah, the Exalted, says:
"And if any one of the polytheists seeks your protection, then grant him protection so that he may hear the words of Allah. Then deliver him to his place of safety." (9:6)

13 A Muslim is not to swear or speak ill of the non-Muslims' faith. Allah, the Exalted, says:
"And do not insult those they invoke other than Allah, lest they insult Allah in enmity without knowledge." (6:108)

14 Allah has ordered that we repay our loans to a non-Muslim. He, the Exalted, says:
"O you who have believed, fulfill [all] contracts." (5:1)

He, the Exalted, also says:
"And fulfill [every] commitment. Indeed, the commitment is ever [that about which one will be] questioned." (17:34)

15 Furthermore, we are encouraged to show kindness and to uphold justice for those who do not share our faith. Allah, the Exalted, says: "As regards those who do not fight you because of religion and do not expel you from your homes, Allah does not

forbid you from being righteous toward them and acting justly toward them. Indeed, Allah loves those who act justly." (60:8)

The Prophet ﷺ also said: "Whoever kills a person who is under a contract of safety in a Muslim country, that person will not even smell the scent of Jannah." (Bukhari)

16 When a non-Muslim resides in a Muslim state, he would receive the welfare services due to any citizen who has reached a senior age. Umar saw an old man who was Jewish and he asked about his condition. He was told that he was from the people who had previously paid the protection-tax. So the Caliph, Umar, told him, "We have not been fair to you. We took Jizyah from you while you were young and now that you are old, you have nothing!" So he took him by his hand till he went to the Muslim treasury, and he gave him some food and clothing. He then told the treasurer, "Find people like him and give them what is enough for them and their families." He then recited the verse: "Zakah expenditures are only for the poor and for the needy." (9:60)

A Muslim is not to swear or speak ill of the non-Muslims' faith.

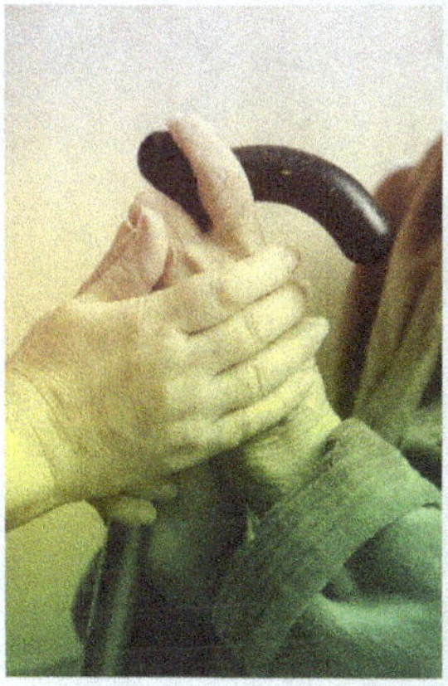

When a non-Muslim resides in a Muslim state, he would receive the welfare services due to any citizen who has reached a senior age.

He said the poor are the Muslims and the needy are those from the People of the Book.

17 Allah has opened the gateway of forgiveness for them (non-Muslims). He, the Exalted, says:

"Say to those who have disbelieved [that] if they cease, what has previously occurred will be forgiven for them. But if they return to hostility], then the precedent of the former [rebellious] peoples has already taken place." (8:38)

18 Wanting good for others is a sign of one's faith. The Prophet ﷺ said to Abu Hurairah: "O Abu Hurairah, be cautious, and you will be the most devoted of people to Allah. Be content, and you will be the most grateful of people to Allah. Love for people what you love for yourself, and you will be a (true) believer. Be a good neighbor to your neighbors, and you will be a (true) Muslim. And laugh little, for laughing a lot deadens the heart spiritually." (Saheeh Ibn Majah)

TOLERANCE OF ISLAM IN PURIFICATION:

All acts of worship in Islam are built upon tolerance, as this is an intrinsic trait in Islam. Allah, the Exalted, says:
"Those who have believed and whose hearts are assured by the remembrance of Allah. Unquestionably, by the remembrance of Allah hearts are assured." (13:28)

All aspects of worship in Islam are in line with one's natural disposition, and one is not burdened beyond his abilities.

No one is overburdened. The Prophet ﷺ said: "Do those deeds which you can do easily, as Allah will not get tired of giving rewards till you get apathetic and tired of performing religious deeds." (Bukhari)

All aspects of worship in Islam are in line with one's natural disposition, and one is not burdened beyond his abilities. A Muslim is not overburdened beyond what he can withstand, even in terms of his acts of worship. Anas saw an elderly man, carried by his two sons, coming to the Masjid. The Prophet ﷺ asked: "Who is this?" They told him, "This man has vowed to walk to the masjid, and he was very ill." The Prophet ﷺ said: "Allah is not in need of this man punishing himself." (Bukhari)

When a Muslim falls ill, Allah will give the person the rewards for deeds that he would have done if he were not ill. The Prophet ﷺ said: "If a person falls ill, or travels, he would receive the rewards of his deeds that he would do if he was healthy." (Bukhari)

A Muslim is not overburdened beyond what he can withstand, even in terms of his acts of worship.

Allah also loves that one takes the approach that is easiest and permissible from that which He has prescribed for Muslims. The Prophet ﷺ said: "Indeed Allah loves that one of you takes the license which He has given (to ease certain matters) in the same degree as He despises it when you do an act which is prohibited." (Saheeh - Albaani)

TOLERANCE IN PURIFICATION:

Purification is a necessity for the majority of acts of worship, and water is used as the medium for this purification.

01 Water is always pure as long as its smell, color or taste does not change.

02 Water that a cat has drunk from is lawful to use for the purpose of purification. Indeed Allah's Messenger said regarding the cat: "It is not impure. It is one of those creatures that lives among us." (Tirmidhi)

03 When water is scarce and/or using water is detrimental to one's health, a Muslim may use the dry ablution instead of water to purify themselves. Allah, the Exalted, says:
"But if you are ill or on a journey or one of you comes from the place of relieving himself or you have had [intimate] contact with women and do not find water, then seek clean earth and wipe over your faces and hands with it. Allah does not intend to make difficulty for you, but He intends to purify you and complete His favor upon you that you may be grateful." (5:6)

04 It is also lawful for a Muslim to wipe over their socks when performing ablution. There are conditions that govern this, but in general, this has been legalized to make it easier for Muslims to purify themselves.

05 All places are suitable for worship. A Muslim can perform prayers in any place except in a graveyard or a bathroom. The area chosen for prayer must also be free from any visible traces of filth. The Prophet ﷺ said: "I have been given five traits no other Prophet before was given. These include that every prophet was sent to his people individually, whereas I have been sent to mankind at large and the land is all a place of prayer so anyone who must perform prayers can perform prayers wherever he is, ..." (Bukhari)

06 If there is a visible trace of filth, it can be removed with water. A Bedouin urinated in the Masjid of the Prophet ﷺ and the Prophet ﷺ said, "Pour water over his urine, for you have not been sent to make things difficult for others, rather to show ease." (Nasaa'ee)

All places are suitable for worship. A Muslim can perform prayers in any place except in a graveyard or a washroom.

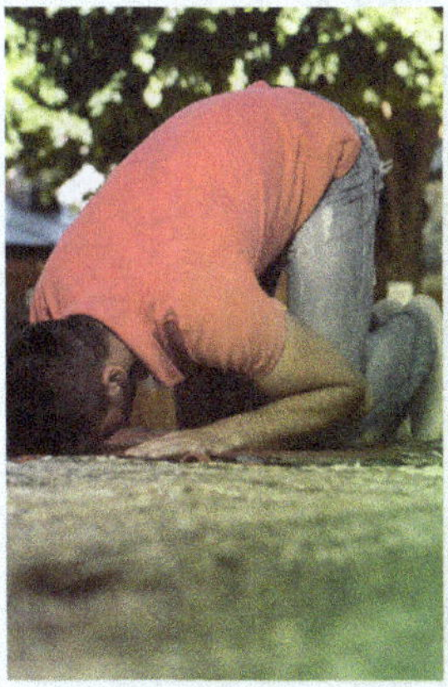

The prayer has many different positions it can be prayed in, taking into consideration one's general condition.

07 Animal dropping of animals whose flesh is lawful for us to consume is not considered an impurity, so if it touches one's clothing or shoes, it would not be considered impure. The Prophet ﷺ was asked about performing prayers in sheep yards and he said it was lawful, but he forbade that one perform prayers in camel stables.

TOLERANCE OF ISLAM IN PRAYERS:

Prayers are the link between a person and God. A person prays to God seeking His Mercy and Forgiveness. Prayer not only is an act of worship but also serves a social function; Muslims from across one community would congregate to pray in the Mosque together. The Prophet ﷺ said: "The first thing a person will be held accountable for on the Day of Resurrection is his prayers; if they are complete, then all his deeds will be accepted." (Tirmidhī)

Prayers are the link between a person and God. A person prays to God seeking His Mercy and Forgiveness.

When one is sick, or there is a heavy downpour, the prayers may be combined as well.

01 A person is to perform the prayers to the best of their ability.

02 The prayer has many different positions it can be prayed in, taking into consideration one's general condition. Allah, the Exalted, says: "And if you fear [an enemy, then pray] on foot or riding. But when you are secure, then remember Allah [in prayer], as He has taught you that which you did not [previously] know." (2:239)

03 When a person is traveling, four unit prayers are shortened to two units each and two separate prayers can be combined at the same time.

04 When one is sick, or there is a heavy downpour, two separate prayers may be combined as well.

05 The prayers each have a beginning and an ending time. The Prophet ﷺ said: "Angel Gabriel led me in prayer at the House of God in Makkah. He prayed the noon prayer with me when the sun had passed its zenith to the extent of the strap of a sandal. He prayed the afternoon prayer with me when the shadow of everything was as long as itself. He prayed the sunset prayer

with me when one who is fasting breaks the fast. He prayed the night prayer with me when the twilight had ended. Finally, he prayed the dawn prayer with me when food and drink become forbidden to one who is keeping the fast. On the following day, he prayed the noon prayer with me when his shadow was as long as himself. He prayed the afternoon prayer with me when his shadow was twice as long as himself. He prayed the sunset prayer at the time when one who is fasting breaks the fast. He prayed the night prayer with me when about one third of the night had passed. Finally, he prayed the dawn prayer with me when there was a fair amount of light. Then, turning to me, he said, 'Muhammad ﷺ, this is the time observed by the prophets before you, and the accepted time is anywhere between the two times (I demonstrated to you).'" (Ahmad and Abu Dawud)

When a person is traveling, four unit prayers are shortened to two units each and two separate prayers can be combined at the same time.

When one doesn't know the direction of the Qiblah, they may perform the prayer to a direction that they think is the Qiblah.

06 When a person is in doubt if they have added or taken away from their prayer, they are to build upon what they are sure of (the lesser number) and then perform an extra two prostrations at the end of the prayer as this would suffice for the element of prayer forgotten. The Prophet ﷺ said: "If one of you doubts in his prayer and does not know how many units he has performed, let him build upon that which he is sure of, and then prostrate at the end of the prayer two prostrations before the end salutation of the prayer." (Bukhari)

07 When one doesn't know the direction of the Qiblah,(2) they may perform the prayer to a direction that they think is the Qiblah. Allah says: "And to Allah belongs the east and the west. So wherever you [might] turn, there is the Face of Allah. Indeed, Allah is all-Encompassing and Knowing." (2:115)

08 It is forbidden for an Imam(3) to extend the prayers and lengthen them when he is praying in congregation. Abu Hurairah said when the Prophet ﷺ used to perform the prayers, he would

---

(2) Qiblah is the direction towards which a Muslim prays; the direction of Makkah.
(3) An Imam is one who leads a congregation in prayers.

shorten them. He ﷺ said: "If one of you prays, let him shorten the prayer for there is the weak, the sick and the old, and if one prays for himself let him lengthen as he wills." (Bukhari)

TOLERANCE OF ISLAM IN ZAKAH(4):

One of the wisdoms behind the duty of Zakah being obligated upon the Muslims is to remove poverty from the Muslim society.

One of the signs of tolerance in Zakah is that it is to be taken from a person's moderate possessions, not the most valuable or least valuable.

One of the wisdoms behind the duty of Zakah being obligated upon the Muslims is to remove poverty from the Muslim society, and to resolve criminal activities that may rise due to an increase in poverty within a society.

01 One of the signs of tolerance in Zakah is that it is to be taken from a person's moderate possessions, not the most valuable or least valuable. The Prophet ﷺ warned his companion ﷺ Muadth saying: "Do not take the most valuable of their wealth as Zakah." (Muslim)

02 The amount of money that one must pay is very small, and it is due only once a year if the minimum requirement is met. If someone has less than the minimal requirement, in that case he is not required to pay.

03 It fluctuates according to one's personal effort. To understand this, take into consideration a farmer who has an orchard of vegetables or the like. In charity, he is obliged to give 10%, but if he watered the orchard himself, then he must give only 5%.

04 If one cannot pay Zakah, it is no longer due upon him. The Prophet ﷺ said: "Only one who is able to pay, shall pay the Zakah." Allah, the Exalted, says: "Zakah expenditures are only for the poor and for the needy and for those employed to collect [zakah] and for bringing hearts together [for Islam] and for freeing captives [or slaves] and for those in debt and for the cause of Allah and for the [stranded] traveler – an obligation [imposed] by Allah. And Allah is Knowing and Wise." (9:60)

(4) Zakah is the obligatory charity a Muslim gives. There are conditions for its obligation, namely that one have the minimum amount saved for an entire year.

05 When one gives it out, they are not losing, but gaining in the sight of God. Allah, the Exalted, says: "Take, [O Muhammad], from their wealth a charity by which you purify them and cause them increase, and invoke [Allah's blessings] upon them. Indeed, your invocations are reassurance for them. And Allah is Hearing and Knowing." (9:103)

TOLERANCE IN TERMS OF FASTING:

When one fasts they would develop discipline in controlling their urges as well as feel the difficulties faced by their less fortunate brothers and sisters around the world. It is also a form of Jihad(5) in which one strives to please Allah.

When one fasts they would feel the difficulties faced by their less fortunate brothers and sisters around the world.

01 It is due to the Mercy of God that only one month in a year is made a time of obligatory fasting upon Muslims. Allah says: "The month of Ramadan [is that] in which was revealed the Qur'an, a guidance for the people and clear proofs of guidance and criterion. So, whoever sights [the new moon of] the month, let him fast it."(2:185)

02 The time for fasting is set, and does not continue in the night. Fasting is only to be done during the day. Allah says: "It has been made permissible for you the night preceding fasting to go to your wives [for intimate relations]. They are clothing for you and you are clothing for them. Allah knows that you used to deceive yourselves, so He accepted your repentance and forgave you. So now, have relations with them and seek that which Allah has decreed for you. And eat and drink until the white thread of dawn becomes distinct to you from the black thread [of night]. Then complete the fast until the sunset. And do not have relations with them as long as you are staying for worship in the mosques. These are the limits [set by] Allah, so do not approach them. Thus does Allah make clear His Command to the people that they may become righteous." (2:187)

The time for fasting is set, and does not continue in the night. Fasting is only to be done during the day.

(5) This term simply means striving to serve the purposes of God on this earth

03 It is unlawful for one to fast continuously, throughout the day and night, without breaking the fast. The Prophet ﷺ forbade this saying: “There is no continuous fasting in Islam.” (Bukhari)

04 The reward of fasting is so great in the sight of Allah. The Messenger of Allah ﷺ said: “Allah said, ‘All the deeds of people are for them, except fasting, which is for Me, and I will give the reward for it.’ Fasting is a shield or protection from the fire and from committing sins. If one of you is fasting, he should avoid sexual relations with his wife and quarreling, and if somebody should fight or quarrel with him, he should say, ‘I am fasting.’ By Him in Whose Hands my soul is, the unpleasant smell coming out from the mouth of a fasting person is better in the sight of Allah than the smell of musk. There are two pleasures for the fasting person, one at the time of breaking his fast, and the other at the time when he will meet his Lord; then he will be pleased because of his fasting.” (Bukhari)

It is unlawful for one to fast continuously, throughout the day and night, without breaking the fast.

05 It is lawful for one who is sick or traveling to break the fast. Allah, the Exalted, says: “And whoever is ill or on a journey – then an equal number of other days. Allah intends for you ease and does not intend for you hardship and [wants] for you to complete the period and to glorify Allah for that [to] which He has guided you, and perhaps you will be grateful.” (2:185)

It is forbidden for anyone to burden themselves with more than that which they can bear. Jabir bin Abdullah said: “The Messenger of Allah ﷺ was traveling and he saw a man around whom many were gathered. The Prophet ﷺ asked, ‘What is wrong with him?’ They told him, ‘He is fasting.’ The Prophet ﷺ then said: ‘It is not of piety for one to fast while they travel.’” (Bukhari)

When a woman is pregnant or nursing her newborn, and she is fearful that she would harm herself or her child, she may break her fast.

06 When a woman is pregnant or nursing her newborn, and she is fearful that she would harm herself or her child, she may break her fast, but must make up those days afterward when she can or feed the poor and needy. This is the case for the very old person as well; he may break the fast and feed the poor and needy for each day of fasting he missed. Allah, the Exalted,

says: "Allah does not charge a soul except [with that within] its capacity." (2:286)

07 Whoever eats or drinks forgetfully or absentmindedly or is forced to do so, his fasting remains intact. The Prophet ﷺ said: "Whoever has forgotten and then has eaten or drank [during his fast], let him complete his fast for indeed Allah has blessed that person with food and drink." (Bukhari)

Hajj is obligatory upon us only once in a lifetime. It is a very difficult duty, and were it obligated yearly, we would fail in this duty.

TOLERANCE IN THE PILGRIMAGE (HAJJ):

One of the goals of Hajj is to uphold the belief in the oneness of Allah. We repeat during the Hajj the phrase: "Lab'baika Al'laahuma Lab'baik," which means: "O Allah, we have come to this place only to respond to your call and so that you may be pleased with us. You are the only one who deserves to be worshipped." In Islam, there is no difference between any two people, whether they are rich and noble, or poor and ignoble.

01 It is obligatory upon us only once in a lifetime. It is a very difficult duty, and were it obligated yearly, we would fail in this duty. The Prophet ﷺ said: "O people, Allah has ordained Hajj upon you, so perform the Hajj." One of the men there said: "Is it a duty every year?" The Prophet kept quiet. The man then repeated himself and he replied, "Were I to say yes, the Hajj would become due upon you every year, and you would not be able to do this." (Muslim)

When one is unable to perform this pillar of Islam, it is not due upon him.

02 When one is unable to perform this pillar of Islam, it is not due upon him. The inability here goes back to two matters: financial and physical inabilities. If a person is not financially able, he is not required to perform the pilgrimage of Hajj, and if a person does not have the physical but has the financial means, he is not required to perform it himself. In this latter case, someone can perform Hajj on his behalf and this would be sufficient. It is reported that a man came to the Prophet ﷺ and said: "My father is a very old man and does not have strength to perform Hajj (pilgrimage) or 'Umrah or to undertake

the journey." The Prophet ﷺ said, "Perform Hajj and 'Umrah on behalf of your father." (Abu Dawud)

03 Allah has also given the believer the choice of choosing which of the three styles of Hajj he wants to perform. Although the Prophet performed one specific style, we are not obliged to do exactly this particular one. We can choose the other two forms as well. It would go back to one's condition and what is more convenient for him.

If one fears that he will not be able to complete the pilgrimage of Hajj, he can place a condition on his entry into the Hajj ritual.

04 If one does something that would negatively affect his Hajj, he can make it up with small offerings as mentioned by Allah. He, the Exalted, says:
"And complete the Hajj and 'Umrah for Allah. But if you are prevented, then [offer] what can be obtained with ease of sacrificial animals. And do not shave your heads until the sacrificial animal has reached its place of slaughter. And whoever among you is ill or has an ailment of the head [making shaving necessary] must offer a ransom of fasting [three days] or charity or sacrifice. And when you are secure, then whoever performs 'Umrah [during the Hajj months] followed by Hajj [offers] what can be obtained with ease of sacrificial animals. And whoever cannot find [or afford such an animal] - then a fast of three days during Hajj and of seven when you have returned [home]. Those are ten complete [days]. This is for those whose family is not in the area of al-Masjid al-Haram. And fear Allah and know that Allah is severe in penalty." (2:196)

05 If one fears that he will not be able to complete the pilgrimage of Hajj, he can place a condition on his entry into the Hajj ritual. If this condition is put upon him, he would be able to break his Hajj ritual without any penalty.

06 Performing the Hajj is a cause for the forgiveness of one's sins. The Prophet ﷺ said: "Whoever performs Hajj (pilgrimage) and does not have sexual relations (with his wife), nor commits sin, nor disputes unjustly (during Hajj), then he returns from Hajj as pure and free from sins as on the day on which his mother gave birth to him." (Bukhari and Muslim)

TOLERANCE IN RELATION TO WOMEN IN ISLAM:

Women in Islam have their unique status; they are honored and given many rights. The Prophet ﷺ said: "The most complete of all believers in terms of their manners and faith are the best of them to their wives." (Ibn Hibban)

He ﷺ also said: "Be kind to your wives." (Muslim)

01 A woman is given a dowry when she gets married. She may ask for whatever she wants and it is a duty upon the man to give it to her. Allah, the Exalted, says: "And give the women [upon marriage] their [bridal] gifts graciously. But if they give up willingly to you anything of it, then take it in satisfaction and ease." (4:4)

02 Even if a woman is divorced, she is given her dowry. Allah, the Exalted, says: "And if you divorce them before you have touched them and you have already specified for them an obligation, then [give] half of what you specified – unless they forego the right or the one in whose hand is the marriage contract foregoes it. And to forego it is nearer to righteousness. And do not forget graciousness between you. Indeed Allah, of whatever you do, is Seeing." (2:237)

03 It is a duty upon the man to take care of all his wife's financial needs. It is forbidden for him to be harsh towards her. Allah, the Exalted, says: "Let the women [who are undergoing a waiting period] live in the same manner as you live yourselves, in accordance with your means, and do not harass them in order to make their lives difficult." (65:6)

04 It is the right of a woman to seek the custody of her child if she so wishes. Allah, the Exalted, says: "And the [divorced] mothers should nurse their children for two whole years, if they wish to complete the period of nursing, and during that period the father of the child shall be responsible for the maintenance of the mother in a reasonable manner. No soul is charged with

It is a duty upon the man to take care of all his wife's financial needs.

A woman is not obligated to spend of her own money on household matters, even if she has her own source of income.

more than it can bear. No mother should be made to suffer on account of her child, and no father should be made to suffer on account of his child. The same duties devolve upon the father's heir [in case of the death of the father]..." (2:233)

05 A woman is to be given her necessities so that she is properly maintained. Allah, the Exalted, says:
"Let the man of means spend in accordance with his means, and let him whose resources are restricted, spend in accordance with what Allah has given him. Allah does not burden any person with more than He has given him. Allah will soon bring about ease after hardship." (65:7)

It is the right of a woman to seek the custody of her child if she so wishes.

When a woman is in her menstrual or post-natal period, she is not required to do certain acts of worship.

06 A woman is given her fair share of inheritance. Allah, the Exalted, says:
"Men shall have a share in what parents and relatives leave behind, and women shall have a share in what parents and relatives leave behind, whether it be little or much. This is ordained [by Allah]." (4:7)

07 When a women is in her menstrual or post-natal period, she is not required to do certain acts of worship; she is not required to perform prayers, nor is she required to fast. She is to make up for fasts missed in the month of Ramadan afterward. According to the Prophetic Tradition: Mu'adha said, "I asked A'ishah, 'What is the reason that a menstruating woman completes the fasts (that she abandons during her monthly course), but she does not complete the prayers?' She said, 'We passed through this (period of menstruation), and we were ordered to complete the fasts, but were not ordered to complete the prayers.'"

Also, a woman is not required to perform the farewell circling of Hajj during her menstrual period. The Prophet ﷺ said: "The people were ordered to perform the circumambulation of the Ka'ba as the last rite before leaving (Mecca), except the menstruating women who were excused." (Bukhari)

08 It is not compulsory upon a woman to fight in war. A'ishah reports:

"I said, 'O Messenger of Allah! We consider Jihad as the best deed. Should we not then go for Jihad?' The Messenger of Allah ﷺ said, 'The best Jihad for women is the accepted Hajj.'" (Bukhari)

09 A woman is not obligated to spend of her own money on household matters, even if she has her own source of income. This provision is the duty of the husband.

TOLERANCE OF ISLAM IN RELATION TO FINANCIAL MATTERS:

Finances are the lifeline of a community and very commonly an area from which a lot of contention between people arise. One of the aspects of the tolerance of Islam in this respect is as follows:

01 One is to be kind with his fellow brother when buying and selling. The Prophet ﷺ said: "Allah will have mercy on one who, when buying or selling, is kind and generous." (Baihaqi)

02 When one is unable to repay a loan, Allah instructs us to be understanding of the person's condition. He, the Exalted, says: "And if someone is in hardship, then [let there be] postponement until [a time of] ease. But if you give [from your right as] charity, then it is better for you, if you only knew." (2:280) The Prophet ﷺ said: "Whoever gives the one upon whom a debt is due time to pay it off, he would receive with each day that passes a great reward." (Ibn Majah)

03 Islam asks that a person be generous towards others. The Prophet ﷺ said: "There was a person from a previous nation who didn't do any good except that he would send his servants to reclaim loans given to people in the community. When one of them was unable to repay he would tell them to go easy on that individual. Allah then forgave that person on account of his generosity." (Muslim)

04 Islam encourages one to reconsider his purchase if the seller feels sorrowful for selling what he has sold. The Prophet

When one is unable to repay a loan, Allah instructs us to be understanding of the person's condition.

Islam encourages one to reconsider his purchase if the seller feels sorrowful for selling what he has sold.

ﷺ said: “Whoever returns what he bought to a seller when the seller feels sorrowful for selling what he sold, Allah will cover from him his faults on the Day of Resurrection.” (Ibn Hibban)

05 If a sale is being conducted, the transaction does not become binding until those involved in the sale get up to leave the session in which the buying/selling was discussed. The Prophet ﷺ said: “The buyer and seller have the right to revoke the sale as long as they do not separate from each other. If they both have spoken the truth, they would be blessed in that sale, and if they have hidden faults there will be no blessing in the sale.” (Bukhari)

A sign of the beauty of Islam is that one is to give a gift to those who are present when money is being divided.

06 A sign of the tolerance of Islam is its beautiful system of inheritance. Allah, the Exalted, says:

“Allah instructs you concerning your children: for the male, what is equal to the share of two females. But if there are [only] daughters, two or more, for them is two thirds of one’s estate. And if there is only one, for her is half. And for one’s parents, to each one of them is a sixth of his estate if he left children. But if he had no children and the parents [alone] inherit from him, then for his mother is one third. And if he had brothers [or sisters], for his mother is a sixth, after any bequest he [may have] made or debt. Your parents or your children – you know not which of them are nearest to you in benefit. [These shares are] an obligation [imposed] by Allah. Indeed, Allah is ever Knowing and Wise.” (4:11)

A person may bequeath a certain amount of his wealth after his death.

07 A sign of the beauty of Islam is that one is to give a gift to those who are present when money is being divided. Allah, the Exalted, says:

“And when [other] relatives and orphans and the needy are present at the [time of] division, then provide for them [something] out of the estate and speak to them words of appropriate kindness.” (4:8)

08 A person may bequeath a certain amount of his wealth after his death. Aamir bin Sa’d said that the Prophet ﷺ would visit him while he was sick in Makkah. I told him, “O Messenger of

Allah, I want to bequeath my entire estate for the sake of Allah." The Prophet said, "No." Aamir then said, "Then a half," and the Prophet once again said, "No." He then said a third, and the Prophet agreed, but added, "A third it is, but a third is still too much. It is better that you leave your heirs rich so that they would not ask people to support them." (Bukhari)

TOLERANCE OF ISLAM IN PUNISHMENT:

Islam has legalized a number of legal penalties which, when upheld, guarantee the safety and security of a society.

Islam has legalized a number of legal penalties which, when upheld, guarantee the safety and security of a society. Lives would be saved, and individual honor would be protected. All crimes, regardless of their degree, would decrease drastically or cease completely. Allah, the Exalted, says: "O you who have believed, prescribed for you is legal retribution for those murdered." (2:178)

Allah also says:
"But whoever overlooks from his brother anything, then there should be a suitable follow-up and payment to him with good conduct." (2:178)

Allah says about theft:
"[As for] the thief, the male and the female, amputate their hand in recompense for what they committed as a deterrent [punishment] from Allah. And Allah is Exalted in Might and Wise." (5:38)

Once a person's hand is cut off, it would discourage him and others to take the property of others.

Once a person's hand is cut off, it would discourage him and others to take the property of others.

The punishment of one who fornicates is also mentioned in the Quran:
"The [unmarried] woman or [unmarried] man found guilty of sexual intercourse - lash each one of them with a hundred lashes, and do not be taken by pity for them in the religion of Allah, if you should believe in Allah and the Last Day. And let a group of the believers witness their punishment." (24:2)

This would serve to prevent the breaking apart of families, and having children left without their parents.

If someone speaks ill of someone, such as accusing them unlawfully of being promiscuous, there is also a due punishment. Allah, the Exalted, says: "And those who accuse chaste women and then do not produce four witnesses – lash them with eighty lashes and do not accept from them testimony ever after. And those are the defiantly disobedient." (24:4)

The tolerance of Islam dictates that punishments related to individual rights are not to be implemented unless the person who is harmed wants it to be implemented.

The Shari'ah affirms a general guideline regarding punishment. Allah, the Exalted, says: "And the retribution for an evil act is an evil one like it, but whoever pardons and makes reconciliation – his reward is [due] from Allah. Indeed, He does not like wrongdoers." (42:40)

Allah also says: "And if you punish [an enemy, O believers], punish with an equivalent of that with which you were harmed. But if you are patient - it is better for those who are patient." (16:126)

THESE PUNISHMENTS HAVE A FEW CONDITIONS:

01 The tolerance of Islam dictates that punishments related to individual rights are not to be implemented unless the person who is harmed wants it to be implemented. Otherwise a person who is affected can pull away from this and forgive the person. Allah, the Exalted, says: "And the retribution for an evil act is an evil one like it, but whoever pardons and makes reconciliation – his reward is [due] from Allah. Indeed, He does not like wrongdoers." (42:40)

Whatever relates to God's rights would be not punished as long as a person does not openly announce that he is committing the sin.

02 Whatever relates to God's rights would not be punished as long as a person does not openly announce that he is committing the sin. In addition, if it has not reached the authorities, the sin would not be punished. One would repent between himself and God. The Prophet ﷺ said: "All the sins of my followers will be forgiven except those of the Mujahirin (those who commit

a sin openly or disclose their sins to the people). An example of such disclosure is that a person commits a sin at night and though Allah screens it from the public, then he comes in the morning, and says, 'O so-and-so, I did such-and-such (evil) deed yesterday,' though he spent his night screened by his Lord (none knowing about his sin) and in the morning he removes Allah's screen from himself." (Bukhari)

The implementations of these rules serve noble ends, namely the protection of human rights and the safety of society.

If a person knows that he will be killed if he kills, or will have has hand cut off if he steals, it is certain that he will be deterred from sinning. Allah says: "And there is for you in legal retribution [saving of] life, O you [people] of understanding, that you may become righteous." (2:179)

It may seem to some that the punishments in Islam are very severe. In reality, they are fitting to each crime and would prevent corruption from spreading in society. Imprisonment, for example, has not proven itself a worthy form of punishment. Rather than deterring one from crime, at times it increases one's willingness to commit crime.

Wars in Islam are fought in an honorable way. They are waged in Islam to protect the rights of the oppressed.

It may seem to some that the punishments in Islam are very severe. In reality, they are fitting to each crime and would prevent corruption from spreading in society.

TOLERANCE IN ISLAM TOWARDS PRISONERS OF WAR:

It isn't unexpected to have people differ amongst themselves in matters of religion, economy and personal interests. Allah says: "And if God had not enabled people to defend themselves against one another, corruption would surely overwhelm the earth, but God is limitless in His bounty unto all the worlds." (2:251)

Wars in Islam are fought in an honorable way. Allah says: "And do not be like those who came forth from their homes insolently and to be seen by people and avert [them] from the way of God. And God is encompassing of what they do." (8:47)

Wars are waged in Islam to protect the rights of the oppressed.

Allah says: “And what is [the matter] with you that you fight not in the cause of Allah and [for] the oppressed among men, women, and children who say, ‘Our Lord, take us out of this city of oppressive people and appoint for us from Yourself a protector and appoint for us from Yourself a helper?’” (4:75)

TOLERANCE IN ISLAM REGARDING WARFARE:

Islam is not a religion of terrorism, transgression or oppression. We are forbidden by God to be oppressive.

01 Islam is not a religion of terrorism, transgression or oppression. We are forbidden by God to be oppressive. Allah says: “Fight in the way of Allah those who fight you, but do not transgress. Indeed, Allah does not like transgressors.” (2:190)

02 Allah orders us to revert to peaceful talks when the enemy requests that option. Allah says: “And if they incline to peace, then incline to it [also] and rely upon Allah. Indeed, it is He who is the Hearing, the Knowing.” (8:61)

Allah orders us to revert to peaceful talks when the enemy requests that option.

03 We are forbidden to fight those who do not fight us. God, the Exalted, says: “Except for those who take refuge with a people between yourselves and whom is a treaty or those who come to you, their hearts strained at [the prospect of] fighting you or fighting their own people. And if Allah had willed, He could have given them power over you, and they would have fought you. So if they remove themselves from you and do not fight you and offer you peace, then Allah has not made for you a cause [for fighting] against them.” (4:90)

04 There are many conditions that go hand-in-hand with warfare, to prevent any inhumane action. No person that has not taken part in the warfare is to be killed. As for the elderly, children, women, sickly, those who have dedicated their lives to worship, and those who did not play a role in the warfare; they are to be left unharmed and spared. These are the commands of the Prophet ﷺ. The Prophet ﷺ upon the conquest of Makkah, instructed that those who entered their homes or the home of Abu Sufyan, or tossed aside their weapons would be guaranteed safety.

Abu Bakr later said to the commanders of his troops: "Do not become treacherous, do not imprison the innocent, do not mutilate, do not kill any children, do not kill any elderly or women, do not destroy date-palms, do not cut down trees that bear fruit, do not kill sheep, cows or camels, except if you intend to eat them."

05 Human rights are protected in times of war. It is unlawful in Islam for one to torture prisoners of war. They must be treated well. Allah says: "And they give food, in spite of love for it, to the needy, the orphan, and the captive. [Saying], 'We feed you only for the countenance of Allah. We wish not from you reward or gratitude.'" (76:8-9)

It is unlawful in Islam for one to torture prisoners of war. They must be treated well.

Muslims were quick to uphold these commands. Abu Aziz bin Umair said: "I was among the captives during the battle of Badr, and the Messenger of Allah ﷺ said: 'Treat the prisoners well.' When it was lunch or dinner time, they would give the prisoners bread and good food, while they themselves would simply eat dates." (Mu'jam as-Sagheer)

06 It is also reflective of Islam's tolerance that prisoners of warfare can be freed without ransom. Allah says: "But thereafter [set them free], either by an act of grace or against ransom, so that the burden of war may be lifted - thus [shall it be]. And [know that] had God so willed, He could indeed punish them Himself, but [He wills you to struggle] so as to test you [all] by means of one another. And as for those who are slain in God's cause, never will He let their deeds go to waste." (47:4)

It is also reflective of Islam's tolerance that prisoners of warfare can be freed without ransom.

07 Muslim governments are instructed to treat their non-Muslim subjects in the best manner. The Prophet ﷺ instructed his companions, when they went to Egypt, "When you conquer Egypt, be kind to the Coptic Christians." (Dhahabi)

If we are to look at the letter that was drafted by Umar to the people of Jerusalem when it was conquered by the Muslims, we will find that it said: "I give the people of Jerusalem my word that their churches and crosses will be protected and not harmed. None of them shall be forced into Islam."

Umar could have put any condition he desired upon the people of Jerusalem, but instead of oppressing them, he acted in a way that was representative of the teachings of tolerance in Islam, and was kind and considerate of their basic human rights.

THE TOLERANCE OF ISLAM IN RELATION TO FORGIVENESS OF SINS:

Allah will forgive one's sins no matter how many times one commits it.

The children of Adam (humanity) often commit sin throughout their lives. The Prophet ﷺ said: "All children of Adam commit sins, and the best of the sinners are those who repent." (Tirmidhi)

Satan has promised to mislead the children of Adam. Allah says in the Quran: "[Iblîs (Satan)] said: 'See this one whom You have honored above me, if You keep me alive to the Day of Resurrection, I will surely seize and mislead his offspring (by sending them astray), all but a few!' (Allah) said, 'Go, and whosoever of them follows you, surely Hell will be the recompense of you (all) - an ample recompense.'" (17:62-3)

01 Allah will forgive one's sins no matter how many times one commits it. The Prophet ﷺ said: "By the one in whose hands is my life, if you were not to sin, Allah would have replaced you with a people who sin, and seek forgiveness and Allah would forgive them." (Muslim)

When one repents to God, there is no intermediary between him and God.

02 Allah has opened the gate of forgiveness for the Muslims. He says: "But whoever repents after his wrongdoing and reforms, indeed, Allah will turn to him in forgiveness. Indeed, Allah is Forgiving and Merciful." (5:39)

The Prophet ﷺ said: "Indeed Allah puts out His hand to forgive those who commit sins, so that He will forgive them, until the sun rises from the West." (Tirmidhi)

Allah says: "The repentance accepted by Allah is only for those who do wrong in ignorance [or carelessness] and then repent soon after. It is those to whom Allah will turn in forgiveness, and Allah is ever Knowing and Wise. But repentance is not [accepted] of those who [continue to] do evil deeds up until, when death comes to one of them, he says, 'Indeed, I have repented now,' or of those who die while they are disbelievers. For them We have prepared a painful punishment." (4:17-18)

03 When one repents to God, there is no intermediary between him and God. The Prophet ﷺ said: "A person's repentance will be accepted as long as the death rattle is not heard from him." (Ibn Majah) In another hadeeth, it states: "Whoever repents before the sun rises from the west, Allah will forgive him." (Tirmidhi) Allah says: "And whoever does a wrong or wrongs himself, but then seeks forgiveness of Allah, will find Allah Forgiving and Merciful. And whoever commits a sin only earns it against himself. And Allah is ever Knowing and Wise." (4:110-111)

04 Those who repent sincerely for their sins would have their sins transformed into good deeds by the will of Allah. Allah, the Exalted, says: "Except for those who repent, believe, and do righteous work. For them, Allah will replace their evil deeds with good. And ever is Allah Forgiving and Merciful." (25:70)

Allah addresses us to repent. He, the Exalted, says: "Say, 'O My servants who have transgressed against themselves [by sinning], do not despair of the mercy of Allah. Indeed, Allah forgives all sins. Indeed, it is He who is the Forgiving, the Merciful.'" (39:53)

05 Allah rewards a person on account of their good intention. If a person intends to do a good deed, and does not do it, he will receive one reward from Allah on account of his good intention.

The Prophet ﷺ said: "Allah says, 'If My slave intends to do a bad deed then (O Angels) do not write it unless he does it. If he does it, then write it as it is, but if he refrains from doing it for My Sake, then write it as a good deed (in his account). [On the other hand], if he intends to do a good deed, but does not do it, then write a good deed (in his account), and if he does it, then write it for him (in his account) as ten good deeds up to seven-hundred times.'" (Muslim)

Those who repent sincerely for their sins would have their sins transformed into good deeds by the will of Allah.

Allah rewards a person on account of their good intention. If a person intends to do a good deed, and does not do it, he will receive one reward from Allah on account of his good intention.

06 When one sins, their sins will not be a barrier between them and the mercy of God. In the Prophetic Tradition, it states: "There will remain one man who will be facing the (Hell) Fire and he will say, 'O God! The heat of Hell has burnt me; please turn my face away from the Fire.' He will keep on invoking Allah till Allah says, 'Perhaps, if I give you what you want, you will ask for another thing?' The man will say, 'No, by Your Power, I will not ask You for anything else!'

When one does a good deed, such as prayers, they will receive their reward from Allah and they will also be forgiven of their sins.

Then Allah will turn his face away from the Fire. The man will say after that, 'O Lord, bring me near the gate of Jannah (Heavenly Garden).' Allah will say (to him), 'Didn't you promise not to ask for anything else? O son of Adam! How treacherous you are!' The man will keep on invoking Allah till Allah will say, 'But if I give you that, will you ask for anything else?' The man will say, 'No, by Your Power. I will not ask for anything else.' He will give Allah his covenant and promise not to ask for anything else after that. So Allah will bring him near to the gate of Jannah, and when he sees what is in it, he will remain silent as long as Allah wills, and then he will say, 'O Allah! Let me enter Jannah.' Allah will say, 'Didn't you promise that you would not ask Me for anything other than that? O son of Adam! How treacherous you are!' On that, the man will say, 'O Allah! Do not make me the most wretched of Your creation!' and will keep on invoking Allah till Allah will smile. And when Allah will smile, He would then allow him to enter into Jannah. And when he will enter, he will be addressed, 'Wish for what you want!' He will wish till all his wishes will be fulfilled, then Allah will say, 'You will be given double what you requested.'" Abu Huraira added: "That man will be the last of the people of Jannah to enter (Jannah)." (Bukhari)

When a person experiences sadness or even a sickness, their patience with these difficulties would purify them of their sins.

Allah, the Exalted, says: "And if Allah were to impose blame on the people for what they have earned, He would not leave upon the earth any creature. But He defers them for a specified term. And when their time comes, then indeed Allah has ever been, of His servants, Seeing." (35:45)

THE TOLERANCE OF ISLAM IN RELATION TO SINS:

01 When one does a good deed, such as prayers, they will receive their reward from Allah and they will also be forgiven of their sins. The Prophet ﷺ said: “The five prayers and the Friday prayers till the next Friday prayers are means to purify one from their sins.” (Haithami)

02 The Prophet ﷺ said: “Umrah to Hajj will purify one from sins and protect one from poverty.” (Muslim)

Smaller deeds have great rewards and would efface sin as well.

03 Allah, the Exalted, says: “If you avoid the major sins which you are forbidden, We will remove from you your lesser sins and admit you to a noble entrance [into Jannah].” (4:31)

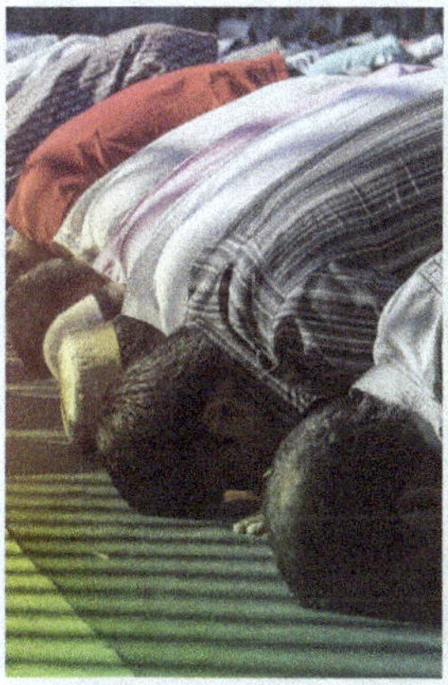

04 The Prophet ﷺ said: “When two Muslims meet each other and shake their hands, their sins will fall like leaves that fall off of a tree.” (al-Mu‘jam al-Awsaṭ)

05 When a person experiences sadness or even a sickness, their patience with these difficulties would purify them of their sins. The Prophet ﷺ said: “Nothing harms a believer except that it would efface his sins.” (Bukhari)

The Prophet mentioned that doing many good deeds will also efface sin.

06 Purification is also a means to rid one from sins. The Prophet ﷺ said: “Shall I not guide you to something that will purify you from your sins and increase your good deeds? They said, ‘Yes O Messenger of Allah!’ He said: ‘Performing ablution when it is difficult, taking many steps to the mosque, and waiting for one prayer after another, for that is like guarding the frontier.’” (Muslim)

07 Smaller deeds have great rewards and would efface sin as well. Abu Hurairah said: “The poor amongst the emigrants came to the Messenger of Allah ﷺ and said, ‘The possessors of great wealth have obtained the highest ranks and the lasting bliss.’ The Prophet ﷺ said, ‘How is that?’ They replied, ‘They pray as we pray, and they observe fast as we observe fast, and they give charity, but we do not have enough money to

give charity, and they set slaves free, but we also cannot afford to set slaves free.' Upon this, the Messenger of Allah ﷺ said, 'Shall I not teach you something by which you will catch up with those who have preceded you, and get ahead of those who come after you? Only those who do as you do will excel beyond you.' They said, 'Yes, Messenger of Allah!' He (the Prophet ﷺ) said, 'Praise Allah (say Subhanallah, Alhamdulillah, and Allahu Akbar) 33 times each after every prayer[(6)].'"

Allah rewards a believer for deeds he guides others to uphold and do.

Abu Salih said: "The poor amongst the emigrants returned to the Messenger of Allah ﷺ saying: 'Our brethren, the possessors of property, have heard about what we have done and they did the same.' So the Messenger of Allah ﷺ said, 'This is Allah's Grace which He gives to whom He wishes.'" (Bukhari)

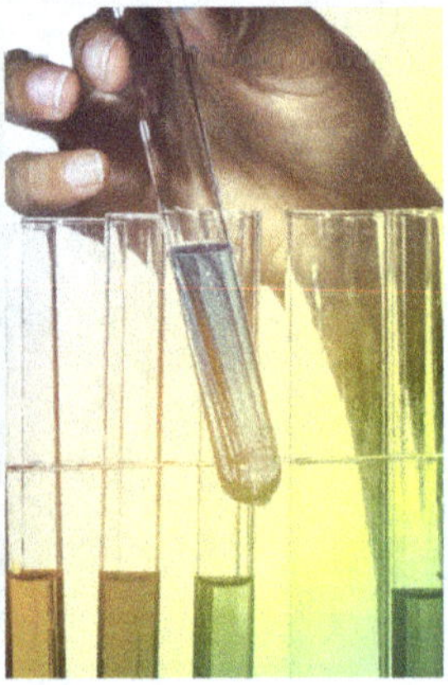

08 The Prophet ﷺ mentioned that doing many good deeds will also efface sin. The Prophet ﷺ said: "Fear Allah wherever you are, and follow up a good deed with another good deed and treat people with good manners." (Tirmidhi)

09 A person came to the Prophet ﷺ after having committed a sin, and said: "O Messenger of Allah, purify me from my sin! The Prophet ﷺ said to him, "Have you performed wudhu?" He said, "Yes." He then asked, "Did you pray with us?" He said, "Yes." He then said, "Go, for indeed, Allah has forgiven you." (Bukhari)

When a person spreads beneficial knowledge in his community, there would be a great reward from Allah for this deed.

TOLERANCE OF ISLAM AND THE CONTINUITY OF GOOD DEEDS:

01 Allah rewards a believer for deeds he guides others to uphold and do. The Prophet ﷺ said: "Whoever calls others to guidance, he would receive a reward equal to those who follow it and those who follow will not have a less reward. Whoever calls others to evil, they will all be punished and the punishment would not be lessened upon any of them." (Muslim)

---

(6) Subhanallah: Far removed is Allah from every imperfection. Alhamdulilah: All praise is due to Allah. Allah Akbar: Allah is Greater..

02 When a person spreads beneficial knowledge in his community, there would be a great reward from Allah for this deed. The Prophet ﷺ said: "When a person dies, his deeds would cease to continue except from three sources: a continuous charity, beneficial knowledge and a pious son who supplicates for him." (Muslim)

TOLERANCE OF ISLAM AND ONE'S DESIRES:

01 When one relieves their desires in the proper way, within marriage, they would receive reward for this as well. The Prophet ﷺ said: "... And ordering with the good is a greatly rewarded deed, and forbidding evil is a rewarded deed, and when you approach your wife, desiring her, you will also receive a reward.' The Companions said: 'O Messenger of Allah would one of us approach his wife, desiring her and receive a reward?' The Prophet ﷺ said, 'Do you not see if he relieves his desire in an unlawful manner, that he will be punished? Likewise if he relieves this desire in a lawful manner, he will be rewarded.'" (Muslim)

When one relieves their desires in the proper way, within marriage, they would receive reward for this.

02 One of the beautiful things about Islam is that normal, average, day-to-day activities transform into acts of worship if done in accordance with the teachings of the Quran and Sunnah, and in remembrance of Allah and His Commands. Eating, drinking, and exercising, when done with the intention of preparing oneself to do that which is ordained by God, would be greatly rewarded. The Prophet ﷺ said: "Whoever spends his wealth in order to maintain his family, he would receive a reward for that." (Bukhari)

One of the beautiful things about Islam is that normal, average, day-to-day activities transform into acts of worship.

The Prophet ﷺ said: "Every Muslim has to give in charity.' The people asked, 'O Prophet of Allah! If someone has nothing to give, what will he do?' He replied, 'He should work with his hands and benefit himself and also give in charity (from what he earns).' The people further asked, 'If he cannot find even that?' He replied, 'He should help the needy who appeal for help.' Then the people asked, 'If he cannot do that?' He replied, 'Then he should perform good deeds and keep away from evil deeds and this will be regarded as charity from him.'" (Bukhari)

TOLERANCE OF ISLAM IN TRAINING:

The method that is used in training and educating others is a method full of wisdom, ease and tolerance. The Prophet ﷺ said: "You have been sent to make things easy (for the people), and you have not been sent to make things difficult for them." (Bukhari)

The method that is used in training and educating others is a method full of wisdom, ease and tolerance.

01 Among the signs of the tolerance of Islam is that the Prophet ﷺ was very kind when people asked him for anything, even if it was the most unexpected of requests. A young man once came to the Prophet ﷺ and asked him: "O Prophet of Allah, allow me to fornicate." The Prophet ﷺ said: "Do you wish this for your mother?" He said, "Of course not!" "Likewise, people will not want this for their own mothers." He said to him, "Do you wish it for your daughter?" He said, "Of course not!" He said, "The same goes for other people's daughters. They would not want this!" He said, "Do you wish it for your sisters?" He said, "Of course not!" He said, "Likewise, people would not this for their sisters." He asked him, "Would you like this for your aunt?" He said, "Of course not!" He said, "Likewise, people would not like this for their aunts." The Prophet ﷺ then placed his honorable hand on the young man's chest and prayed for him, saying: "O Allah forgive him his sin and purify his heart and make him chaste." (Haithami)

Among the signs of the tolerance of Islam is that the Prophet was very kind when people asked him for anything, even if it was the most unexpected of requests.

02 Anas b. Malik reported: "While we were in the Mosque with Allah's Messenger ﷺ, a desert Arab came in and began to urinate in the Mosque. The Companions of the Messenger ﷺ said: 'Stop, stop!' The Messenger of Allah ﷺ said, 'Don't interrupt him. Leave him alone.' They left him alone, and when he finished urinating, Allah's Messenger ﷺ called him and said, 'These mosques are not places meant for urine and filth, but are only for the remembrance of Allah, prayer, and the recitation of the Qur'an.' [The narrator] said that [the Prophet ﷺ] then gave orders to one of the people who brought a bucket of water and poured it over the area where the man had urinated." (Bukhari)

CONCLUSION:

As you read through this book, you will see the evident traits of tolerance and ease in all the teachings of Islam. The Prophet ﷺ said: "Do not belittle any aspect of goodness, even if you are to smile in the face of your brother." (Muslim)

The Prophet ﷺ also said: "The most beloved of people to Allah are those who can benefit others the most. The most beloved of deeds to Allah is to bring happiness to another Muslim, or to help him in a dire situation, or to help him pay off his debt or to suffice him with food. To help out someone in need is more beloved to me than to seclude myself for an entire month in my Mosque in Madinah for the sake of worship. Whoever is able to control their anger, Allah will safeguard their honor, whoever is able to control his emotions when he can inflict damage upon the one who is in front of him, Allah will fill his heart with hope on the Day of Resurrection." (Haithami)

The Prophet ﷺ said: "The most beloved of people to Allah are those who can benefit others the most."

After having read all of these beautiful statements and witnessing the gentleness upon which Islam was founded, I genuinely hope that you will not hold the actions of a small minority of ignorant Muslims against Islam. And lastly, it is hoped that this book will be an important stepping stone in your search for the truth.

THE MESSENGER OF GOD MUHAMMAD

An account of the life of Prophet Muhammad (peace be upon him). The book introduces us to the Prophet's noble character, his humble life and his conduct with his family at home, his companions and all people in society. It tells us how he strove to fulfil the task God assigned to him and contemplates how he dealt with his enemies, the exceptional magnanimity he showed to all and his simple, but highly effective, method of advocating his message.

THE KEY TO UNDERSTANDING ISLAM

This book explains how Islam is a code of living that covers all aspects of life. It comprises a set of acts of worship which play important roles in placing morality on a solid foundation and strengthening good qualities in people so that they are keen to follow the right path. The book cites many examples and speaks about the importance Islam attaches to knowledge. It mentions a number of recent scientific discoveries that the Qur'an has referred to 14 centuries ago.

THE MESSAGE OF ISLAM

The Message of Islam begins by reminding the reader that Islam, its worship, the rules governing people's transactions and all its teachings have always remained the same as they were taught by Prophet Muhammad (peace be upon him). No change or alteration has been introduced into the religion, though some Muslims have changed. The book discusses and sheds light on a number of rights to which Islam attaches great importance.

ISLAM IS THE RELIGION OF PEACE

Islam is the Religion of Peace, shows with perfect clarity that Islam is the religion of peace and that the spread of Islam means the spread of peace throughout the world. Muslims must always be true to their promises and covenants and treat others with justice and compassion.

EASE AND TOLERANCE IN ISLAM

This book explains that Islam admits no rigidity and making things easy is a general feature of all aspects of the Islamic faith. It is a religion God revealed that can be implemented by people with different failings, feelings and abilities. Islamic law takes all this into account and addresses human nature and appeals to it. God says: "He has laid no hardship on you in anything that pertains to religion." (22: 78)

HUMAN RIGHTS IN ISLAM

Human rights in Islam are outlined in the Qur'an and the teachings of Prophet Muhammad (peace be upon him). They aim to make man lead a life of compassion and dignity, so that he acquires all good qualities and deals with others in the best manner. The book clarifies the misconceptions that are often expressed regarding the different aspects of freedom and responds to criticism in a calm and objective way.

BILAL THE ABYSSINIAN

This book tells the history of Bilal ibn Rabah, a former slave who became a companion of the Prophet. The book expounds Islam's attitude to racial discrimination, highlighting significant events that show the Prophet took care of many of those who were persecuted, protected them and gave them their rightful status in the Muslim community.

THE PATH TO HAPPINESS

The Path to Happiness explains that the way of life Islam provides for its followers is divine and intended to ensure that people enjoy real happiness in this present life and in the life to come. Islam establishes the concept of true and everlasting happiness, which makes Muslims aspire to the sublime through obedience of God and earning His pleasure.

WOMEN IN ISLAM

This book discusses the status of women prior to Islam and how women were ill-treated and humiliated in many cultures. It explains how Islam put an end to all this injustice, established women's rights and gave women their rightful status.

ROMANCE IN ISLAM

This book highlights the great importance Islam attaches to love. It shows that the love of God is the best and the most noble love. When it is rooted in a person's heart, it sets that person's behaviour on the right footing, elevates his emotions and feelings and removes selfishness. A person who truly loves God extends feelings of love and compassion to all creatures.

ISLAMIC PERSPECTIVE ON SEX

This book discusses the Islamic approach to sex and how to satisfy the sexual desire in the proper and beneficial way. The proper way to satisfy sexual desire is within marriage and according to Islam, marriage is a necessity for the individual to achieve personal fulfilment. For society, marriage is the way to progress, development and stability.

JESUS IN THE QURAN

After first discussing people's need to receive the divine message through prophets, this book relates the story of Jesus, son of Mary (peace be upon him). It starts well before his birth, then goes on to discuss his message and the opposition he had to endure. The book also discusses the Qur'anic account of Jesus, which makes clear that he enjoys a very high position with God Almighty.

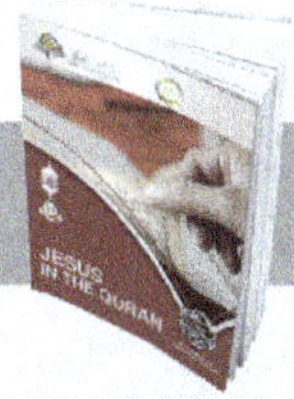

GLAD TIDINGS

Glad Tidings explains the nature of Islam and clarifies the error of people who rely on information on suspect sources. The book highlights the main features of Islam and tells everyone who embraces Islam that God erases all their past sins and errors. As the Prophet makes clear: "Islam wipes away all past sins."

MY FIRST STEPS IN ISLAM

This book explains for non-Muslim readers how to embrace Islam and shows that this does not require much effort. To new Muslims, the book explains the essential elements of Islam and outlines the character of Prophet Muhammad, his qualities and the message he delivered to mankind. It goes on to discuss the various acts of worship Muslims are required to offer, as well as their purposes and significance.

THE PURITY

Under Islam, the concept of purification is not limited to personal and physical purity; it includes purifying oneself of sin and all disobedience of God. This book discusses the detailed rules of physical purification, including ablution, grand ablution, the removal of impurity, dry ablution, etc.

HISN Al-MU'MIN

Hisn Al-Mu'min speaks of the causes of reversals and misfortunes that people encounter. It highlights how one can ensure the protection and preservation of God's favours and blessings, as well as preventing harm and reducing the effects of personal tragedies and calamities. The book teaches the ways and means to fortify oneself against the effect of such tragedies, the most important being remembrance of God and glorifying Him at all times. This book explains the best forms of such remembrance and glorification.

THE BEGINNING AND THE END

Questions of the creation, existence and progress of the universe have been raised by communities throughout the ages. Yet from its earliest days, Islam addressed these questions in a most direct and clear way. This book explains that the ultimate objective of creation is for all creatures to submit themselves to God and worship Him alone. All aspects of life in the universe inevitably end in death then will be brought back to life on the Day of Resurrection when they receive due recompense for their actions.

EVERY RELIGIOUS INNOVATION

This book defines and explains the various types of deviation from the essence of Islam and its true teachings. It reveals the negative consequences of deviation on Muslims and their life and how deviation is bound to give non-Muslims a distorted view of Islam. Finally, the book describes the role of Muslims in discarding all deviation, according to their abilities.

www.ingramcontent.com/pod-product-compliance
Lightning Source LLC
Chambersburg PA
CBHW080243170726
48282CB00031B/1182
9788119946327